Decoys

And Proven Methods
for Using Them

Wade Bourne

Ducks Unlimited, Inc.
Memphis, Tennessee

Book design: Saxon Design
Illustrations and dust jacket design: Monte Clair Finch

Published by Ducks Unlimited, Inc.
L. J. Mayeux, President
Julius Wall, Chairman of the Board
D. A. (Don) Young, Executive Vice President

ISBN: 1-57223-392-3

Published September 2000

Ducks Unlimited, Inc.

The mission of Ducks Unlimited is to fulfill the annual life cycle needs of North American waterfowl by protecting, enhancing, restoring, and managing important wetlands and associated uplands. Since its founding in 1937, DU has raised more than $1.3 billion, which has contributed to the conservation of over 9.4 million acres of prime wildlife habitat in all fifty states, each of the Canadian provinces, and in key areas of Mexico. In the U.S. alone, DU has helped to conserve over 2 million acres of waterfowl habitat. Some 900 species of wildlife live and flourish on DU projects, including many threatened and endangered species.

Library of Congress Cataloging-in-Publication Data

Bourne, Wade.
    Decoys and proven methods for using them / by Wade Bourne.
    p. cm.
    ISBN 1-57223-392-3 (hardcover : alk. paper)
    1. Decoys (Hunting)   I. Title.
SK335 .B68 2000
799.2'44--dc21

                                        00-060330

To Becky, Hampton, and Haley,
who fill my life with abounding joy.

Call to Action

The success of Ducks Unlimited hinges upon each member's personal involvement in the conservation of North America's wetlands and waterfowl. You can help Ducks Unlimited meet its conservation goals by volunteering your time, energy, and resources; by participating in our conservation programs; and by encouraging others to do the same. To learn more about how you can make a difference for the ducks, call 1-800-45-DUCKS.

Contents

Acknowledgments

Many expert waterfowlers provided assistance in researching this book, and without their input, Decoys and Proven Methods for Using Them wouldn't have been possible. I extend sincerest thanks to all hunters mentioned in the following chapters. These men are true masters at decoying ducks and geese, and I admire their expertise and appreciate their willingness to share it with others.

Special thanks go to Dick Gazalski, Larry Smittle, Bob Holmes, Chuck Petrie, Charles Frank, Gary Koehler, and Art DeLaurier, Jr. These men went beyond the call of duty in lending their knowledge, being sounding boards, and passing on leads for additional information. Also, graphics designer Monte Clair Finch of Ducks Unlimited displayed unbounded patience in placing every decoy in every spread in just the right place.

I extend affectionate recognition to friends with whom I've slogged mudflats, paddled backwaters, waded flooded timber, and lain in frozen grainfields over nearly four decades of waterfowling. Without partners to share the elation of successes and the disappointment of failures, duck and goose hunting wouldn't be nearly as much fun. My partners include Don Wright, Wayne Clark, Phil Sumner, Don Buck, Tommy Akin, Ernie Briggs, Lane Lyle, Steve Fugate, Mike Boatwright, and Jeff Lannom. God bless them for their optimistic spirits and their love of adventure!

One other hunting partner with whom I've shared many days in the blind is my brother Joe Bourne, a good shot and a great companion. I hope we can spend much of our collective futures together keeping watch over a decoy spread.

Endearing love goes to my wife, Becky, who puzzles over my compulsion to chase waterfowl, but who is also a good sport about it; to my children, Hampton and Haley; and to my parents, Joe and Lucile Bourne, who fostered my love for hunting.

And last and most important, I give praise to God for the perfection of His works and for the stewardship He commits to those of us who love the outdoors. From no other source could come such beauty as a dawn sky full of ducks or geese! May we never fail in our obligation to preserve the natural treasures with which He entrusts us.

Introduction

I will never forget that morning of glory so many years ago on the Ohio River, just a few miles upstream from its convergence with the mighty Mississippi. The river was rising from heavy rains upstream, and water was spilling into bordering fields of corn and soybeans. The breeze was brisk from the northwest. The temperature was in the high twenties, the sky icy blue. And mallards were present in greater abundance than I'd ever seen.

Usually we'd hear them before we'd see them, jetlike sounds of wind rushing under outstretched wings. Then we'd locate the ducks in the bright sky and call to them, and they'd sail downwind, then turn and glide back toward our spread. Soon they'd be dangling in midair, picking out landing spots.

My two partners and I filled our limits in short order, then watched spellbound as flight after flight poured in from the blue pitcher of sky. It seemed as though the whole flyway had found its way to our decoys. That morning and the sheer ecstasy it brought us will stay with me forever.

For hunters, there is some undefinable magic in luring wildfowl in close over a well-placed decoy spread. There is exhilaration, an adrenaline rush, and a special satisfaction in this accomplishment. When ducks or geese circle and scan carefully for any hint of deception, then commit to final approach, the moment of truth has arrived.

Decoys

I've never quite understood why this experience is so mesmerizing. Perhaps it's because hunting for ducks and geese is more intricate than hunting for other game. There is so much work involved, and so many elements have to fall into place. To be successful, waterfowl hunters must find a good spot, then be there when the birds are moving. They must conceal themselves effectively. They must deploy decoys realistically enough to deceive birds that are wary by instinct. They must call naturally and persuasively. And finally, they must be able to hit moving targets with a shotgun.

Knitting all these elements together is a great accomplishment—indeed, an art form! Hunters most successful in waterfowling are those who are savvy, who are imaginative, who have abounding energy, who are willing to spend their money, who are persistent, who are good athletes, who are hardy, and who are sometimes foolhardy.

My introduction to waterfowling came at an early age. Carl Flair, a friend of my father, invited me on a duck hunt on Kentucky Lake near my Tennessee home. I was twelve years old, and hunting was in my genes. My father was a quail hunter, and I'd tagged behind him since I was old enough to burrow through briars and broomsedge.

But that morning on the big water, Mr. Flair drew back the curtain to a new, exciting world of decoys, blinds, calling, and birds sailing in. I don't remember bagging a duck on that hunt, but the older hunters splashed several. I was enthralled at the mallards' size (much bigger than quail!) and their colors. I was like a Lab puppy mouthing his first warm bird.

My next waterfowl hunt came four years later, after I was old enough to drive. My friend Lane Lyle invited me to hunt with him, again on Kentucky Lake. His family owned a cabin on the lakeshore. We drove down one afternoon, stayed overnight, then rose before dawn to motor across the lake to an island where Lane had a makeshift blind.

This hunt took place in late December, and a strong northern front had blown through during the night. The lake was choppy as we set out in my friend's Alumacraft. We had a heavy load of decoys and other gear. As the boat plowed through the waves, spray flew over us, then froze in the chill. Our boat grew heavier by the minute from this coating of ice. By the time we beached on Lane's island, the V-hull was close to capsizing. On this second outing, I'd had perhaps my worst-ever brush with disaster while hunting waterfowl. A few more yards or minutes, and the boat would have gone under, leaving us bobbing in life jackets in a very large, dark lake. It's doubtful we would have survived.

But our close call was quickly forgotten in the spectacle that came with daylight. Ducks were continuously trading up and down the lake. We huddled in Lane's blind, our decoys scattered before us in a shallow lagoon. The mallards and gadwalls loved our setup, and we bagged an easy limit by the time the sun warmed the morning above freezing.

This was the day I became a duckaholic. With the independence of a car and the freedom of a schoolboy, I embarked on a waterfowling journey that still continues. In the ensuing thirty-plus years I've had an unquenchable desire for wild, wet places and birds that nest in the Far North and migrate south each winter.

In those years, I've hunted ducks and geese from Canada to Louisiana and from California to Georgia. Many days have provided fabulous shooting; many others have been painfully slow. I've made inseparable friends, shared dozens of blinds, explored hidden holes in marsh and timber, admired capable retrievers, overstuffed on "duck hunters' soul food," spent money I shouldn't have, worked like a slave laborer while neglecting real (money-earning) work-all for the thrill that comes in those fleeting moments just before a flight of birds settles into my decoys. Quite simply, there is no other hunting experience like this one. Other hard-core waterfowlers will know what I mean.

As I write this, I gaze around an office littered with the paraphernalia of my years as a waterfowler: photos of my hunting partners on trips we took to-gether, a framed article about duck calls that I wrote for *Sports Afield* magazine, a stuffed canvasback and cinnamon teal, artwork from years of Ducks Unlimited auctions, a shelf lined with old decoys, my duck call collection, my great-grandfather's double-barrel shot-gun over the fireplace, a miniature pirogue on the window sill, books about duck and goose hunting and waterfowl management, my wading staff leaning in a corner, a camo parka hanging on the coat rack.

I note these items to explain my passion for hunt-ing these birds and also for preserving them and the traditions they engender. Each day as I work, I am comforted by my pictures and calls and other water-fowl trappings. They help me count my blessings. They also remind me that the next season is not far away, and there's much work to be done!

I also mention these items to underscore my enthusiasm for writing this book. Besides informing readers about the mechanics of using decoys, I hope to pass along some of the joy I've gained in the marsh and flooded field and timber. A full bag is a proper goal of any hunt. But more worthy and rewarding goals are being outdoors, sharing simple pleasures with friends,

taking pride in making a difficult shot, watching a retriever go through his paces, finding secret places other
people don't go, and working hard to do a job right.

Thus, as you read and gain ideas about using
decoys more effectively, my desire is that you also
realize that when hunting ducks and geese, "how" is
ultimately more important than "how many." Being a
good sportsman is more important than racking up
a high score. Being a good sportsman entails following
game laws to the letter; doing your part to take care of
the resource; fostering the best traditions of hunting;
and passing those traditions on to the next generation.

This past season my 12-year-old son Hampton
and I spent three days between Christmas and
New Year pursuing ducks on Reelfoot Lake in northwest Tennessee. We hunted freelance-style from my
boat, just the two of us in a cypress brake where the
mallards wanted to be.

When a flight would come in, he knew he had
first shot. "Pick a greenhead," I'd whisper as the ducks
fanned out to land. Then he'd come up firing his 20-
gauge, and I'd shoot cleanup.

What a wonderful time we had! When I'm too
old to wade the mud, I'll remember those three days as
some of the best of my life, and I think Hampton will
do the same. This time he was the young Lab pup
mouthing his first warm bird, and the training took.
Now I've got a new partner with whom to share blinds
and promising sunrises.

May the Creator of birds and backwaters give us
many years to enjoy these pleasures together, and may
He bless you in some like and equal measure.

—Wade Bourne
Clarksville, Tennessee

Chapter I

Decoys
in America

In my mind I can see them, crouched in the reeds
in the mist of early morning, hardly moving or gestur-
ing to each other, but keeping a keen eye on the open
water just a few feet away. They are dressed in animal
hides and clutching bows and arrows, holding them
upright and ready to draw. This morning they have
more than casual hope that a few canvasbacks, redheads, or other ducks will swim close enough for a shot.

That's because these Native Americans have a
ruse: a small number of duck imposters—tule reeds
woven together, shaped, then covered with skin and
feathers to resemble live birds. These hunters are aware
of wild ducks' penchant to join others of their kind,
and some inventive tribesman has conjured this notion
of using fake ducks to lure them into killing range. He
has fashioned these decoys from materials readily
available to him.

These hunters, members of the Tule Eaters tribe,
lived approximately two thousand years ago in the
Humboldt Sink area of west-central Nevada. Whether

or not their creations worked is lost to the ages. What is not lost, however, is the hard evidence of their handiwork. In 1924, anthropologists M. R. Harrington and Llewellyn L. Loud, working on an excavation for the Museum of the American Indian in New York, unearthed a basket of 11 canvasback decoys that had been carefully wrapped and buried for two millennia in Lovelock Cave. (The age of the decoys was ascertained through radiocarbon dating tests in 1984.) This is the first documented use of decoys by waterfowl hunters.

Since then, and primarily from the U.S. colonial period to today, the manufacture and use of decoys have become both an integral part of waterfowl hunting and a unique segment of American folk culture. Through-

©M. R. Harrington, 1924. Courtesy of The National Museum of the American Indian, Smithsonian Institution.

In 1924, anthropologist L. L. Loud helped unearth these 2,000-year-old canvasback decoys in New Mexico.

out history decoys have been like the Tule Eaters' canvasbacks: a combination of practical innovation and artful craftsmanship. Decoys were and continue to be made primarily for luring ducks and geese to the gun. The fact that some have found their way onto auction blocks and collectors' shelves are testimony to their makers' talents.

Being aware of the history of waterfowl decoys won't help you bag more ducks and geese. However, such an awareness will further your understanding and enjoyment of the sport. It will also afford you an historic basis for how decoys, and waterfowl hunting itself, evolved to the twenty-first century. For a waterfowler, learning about the history of decoys is like an art student studying the Old Masters. Knowing a subject's past provides more feeling and more appreciation for its present.

Early History of Decoys

The word "decoy" is a shortened version of the Dutch word "EndeKooy," which was a cage-type trap for snaring wildfowl. Nets were rigged over small streams and ditches, and ducks especially were lured or driven into these EndeKooys, where they were then captured by hand and slaughtered for the table. Sometimes semi-tame ducks (the original live decoys) were used to entice their wild cousins into these traps. Besides Holland, trapping ducks was also practiced in England, as verified through popular literature of the early 1800s.

No one really knows when or where waterfowl decoys—the floating, fake kind—were first used, or who made them. Some archivists believe decoys originated in ancient Egypt. What is certain, however, is that

Decoys

Native Americans used crude decoys for centuries before Europeans even knew this continent existed. Proof
of this rests in the Tule Eaters' reed-and-skin canvasbacks. Other natives are known to have fashioned decoys from mud clumps or rocks, sometimes adorning
them with sticks, feathers, or skins for extra realism.

The first recorded use of modern decoys stems
from the U. S. colonial period. Some hunters from this

era made decoys
from cloth and
leather, but these
couldn't stand up to
battering from wind
and waves. Others
fashioned "root-
head" decoys by
whittling chunks of
wood with limbs or
roots growing out of

This early wooden mallard decoy
shows patina of many years' use.

them to look like ducks. These wooden decoys proved
durable enough to withstand the elements, and they
had ample flotation to ride high in the water like real
wildfowl. Thus wood became the material of choice for
decoy makers until the mid-1900s. Favorite woods for
carving "blocks" were white pine, white and red cedar,
cypress, ash, tupelo, and other species with the required
qualities of softness and buoyancy.

Decoys of this early era were made strictly for
hunting purposes. Their carvers had little time for art
and no notion of themselves as folklorists. Instead, they
were seeking a way to put more meat on the table.
They learned that ducks and geese were easier to shoot
by luring to decoys than by stalking or pass shooting.

In a sense, the history of modern decoys parallels
that of the settlement and spread of European society

in North America. Decoys were first used along the New England coast and in Maryland's and Virginia's brackish marshes and estuaries. They were mostly made by men who spent their lives fishing, trapping, and hunting for the commercial markets of the expanding cities of the Northeast. These outdoorsmen were keenly aware of what live birds looked like, and they reproduced a wide variety of very realistic species in wood: black ducks, canvasbacks, scoters, mergansers, etc.

As Americans pushed westward and settled areas of great waterfowl concentrations, new centers of decoy production sprang up: the Great Lakes, the Illinois River valley, the Louisiana marsh, California's pothole country. Again, craftsmen in these areas carved decoys for local use, and they concentrated on species prevalent where they lived — mallards, pintails, canvasbacks, teal, Canada geese. Some guides and market hunters whittled decoys for their personal use only. Others carved in order to supplement their incomes as farmers, furniture makers, blacksmiths, barbers. These men were good with their hands and with tools, and they could make

Hand-carved decoys like these are both functional lures for waterfowl and detailed works of folk art.

©Gary Koehler

a few extra dollars chopping and whittling decoys in their spare hours.

During this era, live decoys, particularly English callers (small, raucous domestic ducks that resembled mallards), were legal and widely used by both commercial and sport hunters. However, live decoys required year-round feeding and care, whereas wooden decoys could be stacked in a shed and forgotten from the end of one hunting season to the beginning of the next. Thus the convenience of wooden decoys led to their adoption by all but the most ardent waterfowlers.

As the U.S. population grew and more hunters took up sport hunting of ducks and geese, a new industry arose to satisfy their demand for decoys. Factory decoys became available in the mid-1800s, and the decoy business grew rapidly in the last half of this century. Three of the largest operations sprang up in Michigan: the George Peterson company, the J. N. Dodge Company, and the Mason Decoy Factory. These and dozens of smaller factories mass-produced wooden decoys with machine-operated lathes. These decoys were more affordable—and just as effective—as hand-carved decoys. Thus they became the choice for most waterfowlers throughout the continent.

Still, the hand-carvers persisted, turning out decoys for small, mostly local clientele. These decoys embodied their makers' skills and the overall style of their home region. Chesapeake Bay decoys were different from Illinois River valley decoys, which were different from Louisiana decoys. (Chesapeake decoys were heavy and blocky, Illinois River decoys had a higher profile to withstand buffeting by current and ice, and Louisiana decoys were lightweight and portrayed a resting profile for the quiet marsh.)

Three common threads linked the more accomplished carvers regardless of where they lived: a keen eye for natural detail, great artisanship, and seemingly infinite patience. As with painters, singers, and poets, some decoy carvers simply had greater skills, and they outshone their peers. Master carvers such as Elmer Crowell and Joseph Lincoln of Massachusetts, Charles "Shang"

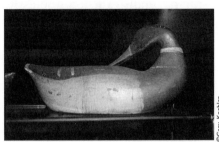

©Gary Koehler

This gracefully crafted decoy imitates relaxed pose of preening mallard to instill confidence in wary ducks.

Wheeler of Connecticut, John Blair of Pennsylvania, Charles Perdew and Robert A. Elliston of Illinois, Clovis "Cadice" Vizier and Mitchell Lafrance of Louisiana, and Richard Ludwig and "Fresh-Air Dick" Janson of California carved and painted decoys with the intricate detail yet simple grace of live birds. Joel Barber, author of the first book on American duck decoys, *American Bird Decoys* (1932), aptly described these decoys of the masters as "floating sculpture."

Thus the decades from the 1870s through the 1940s comprised the golden age of decoy carving in the United States. The astronomical prices that collectors pay today for several master carvers' works attest to their style and quality. Decoys of several carvers now regularly fetch prices in the mid-six-figures range at public auction!

In this era, just as today, waterfowl hunters continually searched for a "better mousetrap," and this led to a broad variety of decoy concepts and designs. Silhouettes, wing-flappers, tip-up decoys, decoys mounted on stakes to simulate flying birds, and decoys that moved and offered different profiles trace their roots back to this period.

Evolution of Modern Decoys

In the 1930s, two things happened that were largely responsible for ushering in the era of modern, ultra-realistic decoys.

First, in 1935, the U. S. government banned the use of live decoys for waterfowl hunting, so hunters were compelled to switch entirely to artificial decoys. When the little English calling suzies were outlawed, a colorful chapter in duck hunting history came to an end.

Second, during this decade scientists in chemical laboratories in the U. S., Germany, and Great Britain were discovering and refining uses for a revolutionary new petroleum-based product—plastic. This, along with the adaptation of other materials such as rubber and papier-mâché, laid the foundation for major changes in the commercial decoy business.

Still, wooden decoys didn't go out easily. Just before World War II, the Animal Trap Company of Pennsylvania bought out at least three other decoy companies, and they set up a huge bank of lathes in a factory in Pascagoula, Mississippi. Their goal was to become the predominant decoy manufacturer in the United States. They would use cheap local labor and abundant tupelo gum forests to produce their Victor label decoys en masse. However, the outbreak of war in 1941 brought about unexpected changes that derailed their plan.

The labor force in southern Mississippi found better paying jobs in war factories. The tupelo trees were needed in the war effort, and the bulk of North America's waterfowlers headed to Europe and the Pacific to pursue more dangerous game. Back in the states, the demand for decoys plummeted. And as the decoy industry declined, so too did the heyday of using wood to make fake ducks.

When the war ended, new materials moved to the forefront of decoy making. Pressed fiber and papier-mâché technologies were used by G&H Decoys, the General Fiber Company (Air-Duk decoys), and Carry-Lite to manufacture goose shells and floating duck decoys. The Victor company introduced a new line of rigid plastic, square-tailed, brightly-colored duck decoys.

In the mid-1950s the first blow-molded, hollow, flexible plastic decoys appeared in Italy. These decoys were much more realistic than their predecessors made from other materials. One of the chief qualities of polyolethane, from which this genre of decoys is made, is its ability to be molded with very fine details. These new plastic decoys thus had individual feathers, curly tailfeathers, wing lines, legs, and other minute features of live ducks and geese.

Blow-molding became the wave of the future for most major U.S. decoy companies. G&H started making hollow plastic decoys in the 1960s. Flambeau followed in the early 1970s, and Carry-Lite made the switch (from papier-mâché) in 1976, when the company was purchased by the Italian credited with inventing blow-molded decoys, Augusto Franceschini. Franceschini subsequently moved Carry-Lite's production to his home country.

From the mid-1970s until now, these companies have used the same basic manufacturing process, but they have made great strides in decoy toughness, paint adhesion, and protection from the sun's ultraviolet rays. Today, blow-molded decoys combine extreme realism and high reliability to offer absolute top efficiency and service.

The other major method for mass-producing decoys today is the solid foam technology used by

Herter's solid foam decoys.

Herter's and a few smaller companies. Polystyrene pellets are put into a mold and injected with steam to cause the pellets to expand and bond, resulting in a solid foam decoy. These solid-body decoys are known for their toughness. They are virtually unsinkable. They are also noted for their graceful ride in choppy water, just like real waterfowl. Their drawbacks are their weight—noticeably heavier than hollow plastic decoys—and their lack of anatomical detail.

Decoys of the Future

What will decoys be like in coming years? Will they be much different from those available now?

No question, innovations will come, though it's difficult to tell where they will come. They probably won't come in terms of physical appearance. How can today's ultra-realistic decoys be improved? It's hard to imagine decoys being more lifelike than they are now.

Instead, improvements will probably come in motion decoys that make natural movements to attract passing waterfowl. And even larger decoys may lie ahead for use on open water. Decoys are certain to be made from new materials that are tougher, lighter, more resistant to damage from ultra-violet rays, and less affected by expanding and contracting from heating and cooling. New painting concepts will come on line that will eliminate chipping or fading. Perhaps hollow decoys will even be self-sealing in the future. Puncture them with pellet holes and they'll close back up. Who knows?

Whatever comes, decoys will always trace their lineage back to the chopping blocks of Crowell, Lincoln, and Perdew and their fellow craftsmen, and ultimately to the Tule Eaters or Egyptians or whoever first conjured up the notion of making decoys to hunt waterfowl. And through this entire history, the links between decoy makers and their products, from the reed-woven Lovelock Cave canvasbacks to the latest assembly-line decoys, are the same: the live birds that have fascinated hunters for millennia.

Indeed, the future of decoys depends on the future of the waterfowl resource. If duck and goose populations thrive, then waterfowl hunting will continue to be popular, and new pages of decoy history will be written. But should the impact of humankind upon fragile earth grow to the point that the great flights of wildfowl dwindle, then hunting will slip away, and the demand for decoys will do the same.

Duck and goose hunters everywhere must dedicate themselves to preserving the waterfowl resource and all the pleasures and traditions fostered therein.

Chapter 2

Decoy
Types and Styles

Not long ago, while poking around in an old barn on our farm, I found the remains of a stack of Canada goose silhouette decoys a friend and I made more than thirty years ago. We were still in high school, and funds for factory decoys were scarce. I recall hand-drawing upright and feeding patterns on cardboard, cutting the patterns out, then tracing them onto thin plywood. Next we jig-sawed the decoys out, painted them, and nailed on wooden stakes to job them into the cornfields and mudflats where we hunted.

Compared to modern decoys, these silhouettes were crude. Their shapes were far from true: oversized bodies, thick necks, drooping butts, etc. We'd painted them solid black except for white cheek patches and rumps. We failed to use treated wood, and after a few seasons they started falling apart from moisture. These decoys were finally stashed in the barn and relegated to more than two decades of obscurity.

But I also remember how well they worked. They pulled geese like magnets. This was probably because of, rather than in spite of, their large size and solid black color. Honkers could see them from a long distance, and coupled with our pleading Ken Martin calls, these rough-hewn decoys were a strong lure for approaching birds to come and join the party. Many did, and never left.

Today my goose decoys are drastically different. Now I own a few dozen large, full-body decoys that are lifelike in every detail. I have standup decoys for fields and floaters for water. I have stackable shell decoys with removable heads and stakes that can be carried easily and assembled on site. I have silhouettes that are photo images of real birds in several true-to-life postures.

I have an equally broad array of duck decoys. I own floating ducks for water sets and standup full-bodies and stakeout shells for fields and sandbars. I have mallard decoys, pintails, green-winged teal, wigeon, wood ducks, black ducks, coots, and other species. I have standards, magnums, and super magnums. Some decoys have swivel heads for a more realistic look. I have sleepers to communicate to circling ducks that all is well on the water. I have soft, lightweight foam shell decoys for toting into hard-to-reach swamps and sloughs.

Drake and hen green-winged teal decoys.

Flambeau

The point is, modern waterfowlers have a huge variety of decoys available to them. These decoys are more lifelike, more functional, and more durable than ever. They are designed for a wide range of uses. They are also good dollar values. While modern decoys aren't cheap, they last for years with proper care.

So how is a hunter to know what to buy? With all this variety available, how does he gear up decoy-wise for a particular hunting situation?

©Bill Buckley

Even with all the decoys available, some hunter's opt to make their own—as these homemade silhouette decoys prove.

Obviously, many factors are involved in selecting decoys. Where will the hunter be hunting? What species will he be hunting? Will the spread be permanent or portable? If portable, how will the decoys be transported? How much can he afford to spend? Answers to these questions will determine which decoys will best fit a hunter's needs.

The logical way to choose decoys is to learn all you can about them—design specifics, advantages, disadvantages—then make the best match possible considering all the variables. Each hunting situation is specific to its own set of circumstances. For instance, the decoy needs of a walk-in freelancer are totally different from those of someone who hunts from a fixed blind with a large permanent spread.

This chapter will examine the decoy options available to hunters. These include types, styles, materials, sizes, and keel designs. Armed with such information, hunters can decide specifically which decoys they need and how to use them for maximum effectiveness.

Decoy Types

Floating Decoys

Far and away, more floaters are used than any other decoy type. Floaters are available in a broad range of materials, styles, sizes, and species. Following are looks at different types of floating decoys, their advantages and disadvantages, and situations to which each type is best suited.

Plastic hollow-body decoys. These are the decoys most familiar to modern hunters. These are injection molded from various thermoplastic resins by North America's major decoy manufacturers. These decoys have some give in their hollow bodies so they can absorb a moderate amount of crushing pressure without breaking. This pliability also allows them to expand and contract in temperature extremes.

Hollow-body mallard decoy from Flambeau.

These decoys are molded with an amazing degree of realism, with true anatomical shapes, feathers, and wing and beak details of real ducks and geese. They float on the water like live wildfowl. Most are molded with fixed heads, though some have heads that will swivel to the side to add more realism.

Plastic decoys are excellent for a wide range of uses, from big water to small, rough water to calm. Their range of sizes (standard to super magnum) allows hunters to pick decoys suited to their particular spot and style of hunting. They are highly durable. They can be set out in a permanent spread and left all year with little sustainable damage.

The main drawback to plastic decoys is their vulnerability to a misdirected shot. Stray pellets easily penetrate these decoys' soft sides, and water leakage will cause them to list or become submarines. However, the shot holes can be easily repaired.

Hard foam decoys. Hard foam decoys are made by expanding foam beads with heat to completely fill decoy molds. Thus hard foam decoys have solid bodies that make them unsinkable. Stray shot has little effect on them.

Hard foam decoys come in several configurations. Some have metal keels inserted into their undersides to make them self-righting when tossed onto the water. These decoys are fairly heavy and ride well in rough water. However, owing to their weight, they are better suited to permanent spreads or

Durable and steady in rough water, hard-foam decoys are great for open-water spreads.

transporting and setting out by boat. These decoys are not a good choice for backpacking into hard-to-reach potholes. Hard foam decoys with keels run in the moderate to high price range compared to other decoys.

Decoys

Other hard foam decoys have concave bottoms with no keels. These decoys weigh approximately half as much as decoys of the same size with metal keels, so they are much more portable. They can be used on land as well as water, since they will rest level. Conversely, they do not ride as well in rough open water as their metal-keel counterparts. They are substantially less expensive than hard foam metal-keel decoys.

One drawback to hard foam decoys is their inclination to become dented or gouged through heavy use. However, this can be overcome by wrapping hard foam bodies in burlap or a plastic coating to harden their outer surfaces. Such outer coatings add considerably to a decoy's cost, but greatly increase its durability.

Soft foam decoys. Soft foam shell decoys are a blessing for hunters who walk or wade into shallow ponds, marshes, or flooded timber. Their main advantage is their extreme light weight. These decoys in 20-inch magnum models weigh approximately a pound per dozen, excluding anchors. Thus a hunter can easily carry 3 to 4 dozen soft foam decoys in a backpack. Also, these decoys can be stacked or rolled to take up little room in a decoy bag or pack. When rolled or wadded decoys are unpacked, their "memory" returns them to their original shape.

Soft foam decoys move realistically in the lightest breeze. They require less anchor weight to hold them in place. They are very durable—they won't break, chip, crack, or sink. They have multiposition heads for extra realism. They are less expensive than hard plastic decoys.

These decoys also have some disadvantages. They are not as lifelike as plastic decoys, but they are still realistic enough to fool ducks. Heads must be inserted into the shell bodies before you set them out, which takes more time than simply unwrapping anchor strings from around hard decoys. Soft foam decoys must be set on the water by hand; they cannot be tossed out. Moreover, these decoys sometimes flip over in a hard blow.

Synthetic rubber decoys. Blended synthetic rubber is a new decoy material that is available in a standard floating decoy and also in a self-inflating decoy patterned after the old Suc-Duk and Deke decoys. This self-inflater (called Inflata-Coy, from Carry-Lite) is flat and rubbery out of the water. It has a 4-inch metal ring and open hole in its bottom. When held 2 to 3 feet above the water and dropped, this decoy traps air in its body as it falls, then vacuum pressure from the water's surface inflates the decoy into a realistic mallard look-alike. The decoy is anchored by

Carry-Lite's Inflata-Coy self-inflating decoys—portability makes them perfect for long hikes into small potholes.

a standard string-weight attached to a small loop molded into the decoy's breast.

These decoys are very portable; a hunter can carry a dozen in a pocket. They weigh approximately 12 ounces per decoy. They are quick and easy to set out. The synthetic rubber is very durable and holds paint extremely well. This material is also virtually impervious to cold.

The best use for these self-inflating decoys is on small, quiet ponds and potholes where hunters must hike in over a long distance. They should not be used on rough water where waves can break the vacuum seal and cause them to sink.

Cork decoys. Cork is an old standard material for high-quality decoys. Cork is highly buoyant, and decoys fashioned from this pithy wood are unsinkable. Cork's natural resins are rot resistant. Cork has a porous texture that soaks in paint, producing a natural no-glare finish.

Modern cork decoys.

Cork decoys usually have a wooden keel, a wooden or plastic head, and sometimes a wooden tail insert.

These qualities mix together to form a decoy that is very realistic. Cork decoys are heavy, approximately twice the weight of plastic decoys, and their combination of weight and buoyancy yields a natural, no-bobbing ride in rough water.

Cork decoys' main drawbacks are their weight and their cost. These decoys aren't recommended for hunters who freelance on quiet, inland waters. Instead, they're typically used on big water and carried by boat rather than backpack.

Also, cork is an expensive material, and much of the crafting of cork decoys is done by hand—making these the most expensive of all working decoys. Still, they are worth the money for hunters who can afford them and who enjoy their connection to the traditions of waterfowling's rich past.

Wooden decoys. Working wooden decoys are made today only by a few carvers whose well-heeled customers enjoy injecting an element of art and history into their hunts.

Wooden "blocks" by decoy maker Red Mietzen.

Modern wooden decoys, mostly fashioned from white cedar and tupelo, can be very realistic, since carvers can make them in a broad range of poses (high head, low head, preening, sleeping, etc.). These decoys are tough. They are very buoyant (especially those that have been hollowed out). They ride naturally in a chop. But they are priced out of the range of most hunters. Wooden decoys can cost hundreds of dollars apiece.

Full-body Standup Decoys

Full-body standup decoys are for use in fields or on river sandbars, gravel bars, mudflats, etc. Their purpose is to simulate geese or ducks standing or walking on dry land. They are mostly used by goose hunters who hunt in feeding fields. They are also frequently set out next to water close to floating decoys to add more attraction to a shoreline spread.

Full-body standup decoys' main advantage is realism. They are molded and painted with all the physical features of real birds. (Most full-body decoys are bigger than live birds.) Full-body goose decoys come with several head positions— sentry, resting, feeding. On most models, heads and standup platforms (legs, feet) are detachable.

One major drawback to full-body standup decoys is their bulk. Because of their size and

Flambeau

Full-body standup Canada geese in sentry and feeding poses.

weight, they are impractical to carry in large numbers over long distances. Most goose hunters who set a big spread of full-bodies drive them right to their hunting sites in trailers. Also, full-bodies are well suited for large spreads that are set out and left for extended periods.

Frequently, full-body standup decoys are mixed with shells and silhouettes for a combination of realism and a large spread. Full-bodies are usually set in areas that waterfowl are more likely to scrutinize carefully — i.e., around the landing zone, around the callers, etc.

A second drawback to full-body standup decoys is their cost. Top-line full-body geese run $25 or more per decoy. A hunter can invest thousands of dollars in a large spread of these decoys. Full-body standup duck decoys cost $12 to $15 each.

Shell Decoys

Shell decoys are hard plastic half-decoys with hollow bodies and detachable heads. With heads removed, the bodies can be stacked, allowing for easy transport and storage. One hunter can carry far more shell decoys than like-sized full-body decoys.

Hard plastic shells do not float, so they are mostly used in fields and other dry land spreads. Shell decoys may be placed directly on the ground to simulate resting waterfowl, or they can be erected on stakes or leg assemblies for increased elevation and visibility. Also, shell decoys may be rigged on stakes or legs and set in shallow water. (Shells are often used on sandbars, mudflats, or

Flambeau

Shell decoys offer the look of full-bodies without the added weight, bulk, and expense.

Super magnum Canada goose shells and super goose blinds in a field spread.

shorelines adjacent to floating decoys for extra visibility and realism.)

The main advantage of shell decoys is that they offer the look of full-body decoys but with significantly less weight, bulk, and expense. Shells are often mixed into goose spreads with full-body and/or silhouette decoys. Their design allows hunters to set out a large spread with minimal effort.

Snow goose shell.

24

Silhouette Decoys

Silhouette decoys have two dimensions—length and height, but not width. These flat cutouts of geese and ducks stand on stakes, so they are used mostly in field hunting or on sandbars or mudflats. Some duck silhouettes are also rigged with small "pontoons" so they will float on water.

Modern silhouette decoys are made from weatherproof plastic. They are very tough and can be cleaned with a water hose.

These decoys offer an amazing degree of lifelikeness in terms of body postures, head positions, feather detail, sizes, etc. Some are even covered with photo images of live birds for ulti- mate realism. From the side, they look totally authentic. However, viewed from straight over- head, silhouette de- coys disappear!

Silhouettes offer hunters a number of advan- tages. One person can carry a stack of several dozen. Sil- houettes can be set out very quickly— just push a stake in the ground. Their expense is less than

©Bill Buckley

Silhouette decoys look realistic from the side but disappear from the view of geese flying directly overhead.

that of a comparable number of full-body decoys (though modern silhouettes certainly aren't cheap). They also take minimal storage and transport space.

Their main disadvantage is their lack of width. Silhouettes are usually set at different angles so that geese or ducks circling a spread will always have some in view. Some hunters believe silhouettes actually transmit an illusion of movement to circling birds as decoys come into and pass out of their view.

However, if the birds cross directly over the spread, the silhouettes will disappear until the birds fly far enough away to regain a sideways viewing angle. Some hunters feel this "disappearing act" has little effect on working waterfowl. Others, however, won't use silhouettes by themselves. Instead, they will scatter them among full-body or shell decoys so that birds flying overhead will still see something to hold their attention. In this manner, silhouettes are used to "thicken" a spread—to add to decoy numbers without using all full-bodies or shells.

(One "new twist" in silhouettes is decoys with an overhead view of geese or ducks printed on one side. These decoys, lying flat on the ground among a spread of upright silhouettes, provide overhead waterfowl with the illusion of birds directly below.)

Another problem with some silhouette decoys is glare off their flat sides in direct sunlight (early morning, late afternoon). Obviously, such glare is unnatural and will scare incoming birds.

Stuffers

"Stuffers" are the elite members of the decoy world. These are taxidermy mounts of real birds, usually Canada geese. What makes them special is their absolute realism and effectiveness (you can't improve on Mother Nature) and also the amount of care it takes to keep them in usable shape.

Taxidermy regulations no longer allow the sale of stuffer decoys, so they must be prepared by the hunter himself or as a favor from a friend. Stuffers aren't as finely processed and groomed as mounts intended for long-term display. Instead, they are basically goose skins stretched over wire frames and mounted standing up on squares of plywood.

Stuffer decoys are extremely fragile. They must be kept dry. They must be powdered regularly to keep the feathers separate and supple. They must be deloused to keep mites from destroying the feathers and skin. They cannot be set facing downwind where a breeze will ruffle their feathers. They must be stored in an enclosed trailer or bin that mice can't penetrate. They must be transported and stored in racks that protect them from damage. And even with the best of care, stuffers generally don't last longer than a few seasons.

So why all this bother? Because, everything else being equal, Canada geese will work to these better than any other decoys. Stuffers repay their owners for their fussiness by pulling live birds in for close shooting when other spreads aren't producing.

Kites, Windsocks, and Fliers

Kite, windsock, and flier decoys are exactly what their names imply.

Kite decoys are goose or duck kites designed to fly over a spread to simulate a real bird hovering over the decoys. A kite's purpose is to add life to a collection of inanimate decoys on the ground or water. A kite decoy bobbing and turning a few yards above a spread is a magnet for attracting the attention of passing birds.

Kite decoys can be tied to a string or to a long pole, like those pictured here.

Windsock decoys catch the wind and look like moving geese.

Kites may be flown on a string or tethered to a long pole erected in the spread.

A windsock decoy is a lightweight sock patterned after an airport windsock. A stake and head (goose, duck, or crane) support a sock that is attached to an open ring at the decoy's front. The sock is free to turn on the stake so that it can catch wind. Any light breeze will inflate the windsockbody and cause it to oscillate back and forth with a waddling motion. Windsock decoys' purpose is to provide movement and a three-dimensional aspect to field spreads. These decoys are very lightweight and quick to deploy by pushing the stake into the ground with the head facing into the wind.

Fliers are decoys set on tall stakes above a field spread to resemble hovering birds that are about to land. These decoys feature lightweight outstretched wings that flap in the slightest breeze.

Tips for deploying and using kite, windsock, and flier decoys are included in chapter 5.

Flier decoys hover on sticks to imitate landing waterfowl.

Rags

"Rags" is an all-encompassing term including cloth rags, plastic squares, paper plates, and other white, flat, lightweight objects that are scattered en masse across a field to resemble feeding snow geese.

Rag spreads originated in south Texas, where guides spread hundreds of cloth baby diapers to achieve the look of a large concentration of snow geese in a rice field. Rags and other raglike "decoys" were carried into the field in large bags, then scattered to draw the attention of geese at long distances. As rag-spread hunting evolved, hunters began drooping rags over stakes or using plastic goose-head stakes for a three-dimensional effect and more realism.

A numbers game: rags spread over a rice field give the illusion of a large concentration of feeding snow geese.

29

Today, snow goose spreads usually combine rags with shells, windsocks, silhouettes, kites, full-bodies, and other types of decoys. With a rag spread, realism of individual decoys is secondary to sheer numbers, visibility, and movement. Using rags in conjunction with other quick-to-set decoys makes it possible for hunters to set out a huge volume of decoys in a relatively short time. Also, rags are far less expensive than factory decoys, making large spreads feasible from a cost perspective.

Special-effect Decoys

Regular decoys are those with normal body postures and head shapes—upright or feeding. Such decoys usually comprise the vast majority of hunters' spreads. Manufacturers also offer a variety of special-effect decoys to add to a spread's realism and to convince circling waterfowl that the "birds" on the water are contented and safe.

Sleeper Decoy.

One example is the "sleeper" decoy, a floating duck molded with its head tucked back under its wing like a real duck at rest. One or more of these decoys mixed through a spread are designed to communicate tranquility and a lack of any threat to passing ducks and geese.

Feeder Decoys.

Another example is the feeding decoy, resembling the aft end of a duck tipping to feed in shallow water. Several feeders give the impression of an available food source, which should entice circling ducks to land.

A different type of special effect is the "photo-skin" decoy, featuring real photo renditions of live birds. These have been available in silhouette decoys for several years, but they're now making their way into full-body decoys. Outlaw's FotoFeathers are like socks that slide over standard painted decoys to provide nature-accurate realism. Another example is Herter's Millennium mallards, with photo-image bodies but not heads.

Confidence Decoys

Confidence decoys are used in or near a decoy spread to communicate safety to circling ducks and geese. Great blue herons, egrets, gulls, owls, and crows are wary birds that fly away at the first hint of danger. Thus having decoys of these species next to a duck or goose layout supposedly instills confidence in waterfowl that are scrutinizing the spread. The logic is, if everything wasn't okay, these birds wouldn't be here. Also, using one or more confidence decoys adds to a spread's natural appearance.

Great blue heron confidence decoy.

Flambeau

31

Decoy Features

Decoy Sizes

Duck decoys come in standard, magnum, and super magnum sizes. Standard decoys are near the same size as a live duck (approximately 16 inches long). Magnums are larger (approximately 18 inches), and super magnums are larger still (approximately twenty to 22 inches). A dozen standard-size decoys (hollow-body plastic, weighted keel, not including anchors and strings) weigh about 11 pounds, while the same number of magnums and super magnums weigh 15 pounds and 30 pounds.

Goose decoys also come in a range of sizes. Full-body decoys are available

Left to right: super magnum, magnum, standard.

in standard and magnum. Body lengths run from 24 to 33 inches for floaters and 33 to 39½ inches for full-body field decoys. Shell and silhouette decoys measure from 28 to 42 inches.

Why this broad range of sizes? The answer has to do with visibility. Bigger decoys can be seen by waterfowl at longer distances. In many situations, oversized decoys will attract birds' attention farther and faster than an equal number of standard-sized decoys. It's the opposite effect of "out of sight, out of mind." With decoys, "in sight, in mind" is the rule, and big decoys are "in sight" more than small decoys.

Also, years of field-testing have proved that ducks and geese usually show little hesitation at landing with decoys that are bigger than life. (Old Volkswagen Beetles have been used successfully as gigantic decoys to pull Canada geese over long distances.) Waterfowl may not have the depth perception to distinguish unnatural sizes from natural ones, or more likely, they lack the reasoning power to understand that oversized ducks and geese are unnatural. The reason isn't important to a hunter. Results are what matter, and it's proven that waterfowl respond well to oversized decoys.

So why not use oversized decoys in every setup? Why do decoy manufacturers even offer standard sizes?

Answers to these questions have to do with cost, transporting decoys, and practical use. In one major retailer's catalog, a dozen standard decoys is listed for $70. A dozen magnums in the same brand and style cost $90, while a dozen super magnums cost $150. Also, in these same decoys, standards are less than half the weight of super magnums.

Now assume you plan to hunt a quiet slough or pond where ducks will be up close before you see them, or before they see the spread. In this case, standard decoys are more practical. Ducks can spot them easily, and they are much lighter to backpack to the hunting spot. Plus they cost less than half as much as the bigger decoys. Why pay extra if you don't need to?

On the other hand, consider that you're hunting out of a boat on a big marsh or river, and you're trying to attract ducks from longer distances. In this case, size and weight aren't important factors in transportation, since the boat is serving this purpose. Here magnum decoys or super magnums are the logical choice for the greater visibility they provide.

The same is true for setting out a permanent spread. Not having to put out and pick up decoys every day makes using larger decoys more practical.

One more situation when magnum or super magnum decoys may be better is when you're competing with other hunters for waterfowl's attention. It is broadly accepted that a spread with more and bigger decoys will outdraw a spread with fewer and smaller decoys.

Thus hunters must make their own value judgments as to which size decoys to use. If cost and weight are important factors, and if ducks are likely to be working close, standard sizes will be sufficient. If long-range visibility is crucial, and the hunter is willing to pay more and can transport the decoys without undue strain, bigger decoys are better.

I keep two sets of freelance duck decoys rigged and bagged for ready use. One set consists of 36 standard decoys tied with shallow lines and light weights. These decoys are divided into two tote bags. I take these when hunting in shallow floodwaters, timber, or other situations where I expect ducks to be close and where walking or wading might be involved. My partner and I can each shoulder a bag of 18 decoys and walk a long way without undue exertion.

My other freelance spread is used when running big rivers or reservoirs in my boat. This spread consists of 18 super magnum ducks and 8 goose floaters. These decoys are rigged on multi-decoy lines with heavy weights to hold in strong currents or winds. They don't take long to set out, and they offer plenty of visibility over great distances of open water. But heaven help the hunter who shoulders my bag of super magnums and starts hiking across a muddy field!

Decoy Species

Open a decoy catalog and you will see duck and goose decoys in a broad range of species. Puddle ducks are available in mallards, black ducks, pintails, wood ducks, wigeons, gadwall, shovelers, blue-winged teal, and green-winged teal. Diving duck decoys come in scaup (bluebills), canvasbacks, redheads, goldeneyes, and ringnecks. Sea ducks come in oldsquaws, eiders, and scoters. Geese come in Canadas, snows and blues, whitefronts (specklebellies), and brant.

Common sense dictates using decoys to match the species of waterfowl you're hunting. For instance, duck hunters hunting where mallards are predominant should set out mostly mallard decoys. In the early teal season, a spread of blue-wing decoys is appropriate. Wood duck hunters might opt

Wood duck drake and hen.

Flambeau

for "squealer" decoys on timbered sloughs or creeks. In a Louisiana or California rice field, pintail decoys would be a smart choice. The same holds for diving ducks. Hunters going after scaup should use

Pintail drake.

Flambeau

scaup decoys; canvasbacks, canvasback decoys; red-heads, redhead decoys.

This isn't to say, however, that ducks won't work to species other than their own. Hunters routinely take pintails, gadwalls, wigeons, woodies, and other puddlers over mallard decoys. The same is true of bagging other divers over bluebill spreads.

Redhead drake and hen.

Many veteran puddle duck hunters mainly use mallards for the majority of their spread, but they mix in decoys of other species. A few pintail drakes or black ducks scattered with mallards increase the spread's visibility, and add to its realism. Wigeon, gadwall, or teal decoys probably aren't distinguishable enough from mallard hen decoys—especially on bright, high-contrast days—to be noticeable to ducks circling overhead. Still, anything that adds to a spread's realism is worth a try. Having a few "odd" ducks mixed in with a spread of mallards is certainly natural.

A similar deception is to scatter coot decoys around the edge of a spread. Ducks and coots routinely rest and feed together, so the realism of a decoy spread is increased by the addition of a few

Bluebill drake.

coots. Also, the all-black coots add to a spread's visibility from long distance.

Goose hunters should be more species specific with decoys. Canada goose hunters should strictly use Canada goose decoys. Snow goose hunters should set out snow goose decoys, and specklebelly and brant hunters should use decoys of these respective species. This is because geese don't normally land and feed with birds outside their own species. This isn't to say that Canadas, snow geese, and specklebellies don't intermingle. They do, but the typical scenario is for a single or small number of one species to alight with a large number of another, not wholesale intermixing. Hunters hunting an area where two or three species co-exist (Texas, for instance) normally set their snow geese in one group and their Canada or specklebelly decoys apart in another group.

Decoy Keels

Most floating decoys have keels. The exceptions are those with a concave bottom, which creates a vacuum seal between a decoy and the water's surface, holding the former upright. As a rule, these keelless decoys are best in quieter waters, while decoys with keels are suitable for both rough and calm water.

A keel fulfills three functions for a duck or goose decoy. It provides stability in chop, allowing it to ride with natural balance rather than rolling from side to side. It makes the bottom of the decoy heavier than the top. This allows the decoy to right itself after being tossed into the water. And on many decoys, the keel provides the hole or loop for attaching the anchor line.

Most modern decoys come with either of two keel types: weighted or water keel. A weighted keel is one

with weight (usually sand) added and sealed permanently inside the keel. In contrast, a water keel is hollow, with holes fore and/or aft for water to flow into
and out of the keel when the decoy is set out.

Weighted keel decoys are preferable to water keels
in most situations. They are self-righting when tossed
out, and they don't drain water when retrieved and
placed in boat or bag. On the down side, they weigh
slightly more than water keel decoys and are more

Flambeau wigeon weighted keel decoys.

expensive (15 to 30 percent more per dozen). However, their advantages far outweigh these minor disadvantages.

Some water keel decoys can be bothersome to
toss out, since they have a tendency to land and remain
on their sides. To prevent this, these decoys must be
placed upright in the water by hand so that water can
flow into the holes in the keel. Their best use is in a
permanent spread, where they can be set out and left
for lengthy periods.

Other types of keels are used less frequently on
decoys. Wooden keels were attached to many wooden
decoys before plastic came on the scene, and wooden
keels are still attached to some specialty decoys today.

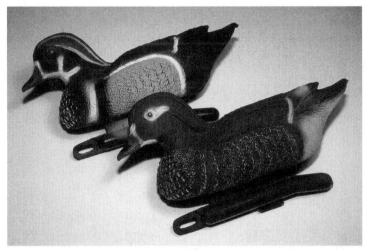

Carry-Lite Aqua Keel water keel decoys.

Strips of metal are also used to weight the bottoms of some wood and hard foam decoys.

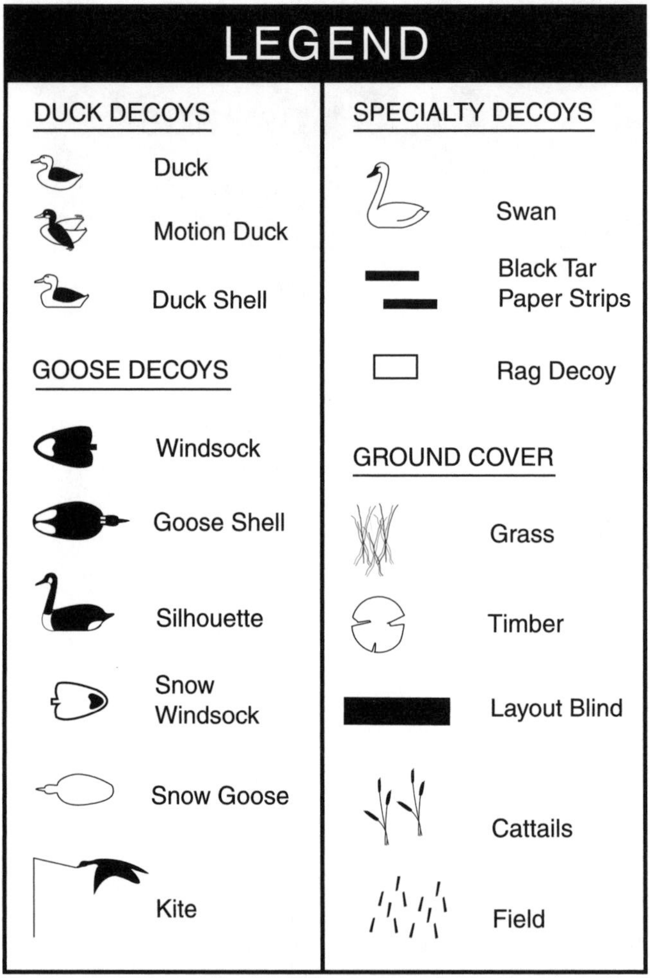

LEGEND

DUCK DECOYS

- Duck
- Motion Duck
- Duck Shell

GOOSE DECOYS

- Windsock
- Goose Shell
- Silhouette
- Snow Windsock
- Snow Goose
- Kite

SPECIALTY DECOYS

- Swan
- Black Tar Paper Strips
- Rag Decoy

GROUND COVER

- Grass
- Timber
- Layout Blind
- Cattails
- Field

The decoys in the illustrations are representational only and are **not exact in orientation or number.** Refer to the text for specific details.

Chapter 3

Duck Spreads

Back in the early 1970s I paid a visit to the late George Soule, who made the famed Coastal Decoy for the L. L. Bean Company in Maine for more than thirty years. George's shop was on Casco Bay in South Freeport. It was rich with the smell and shavings of cedar and cork and the whirring of the spindle lathe carving out decoy bodies and heads.

While showing me around, George entertained me with stories about hunting black ducks in the nearby salt marsh. He related in a thick Down East accent how these birds were extraordinarily wary, and how the slightest miscue by a hunter would thwart all efforts to lure them into shotgun range.

I still recall one story in particular.

"I always used 7 decoys," George explained. "The ducks wouldn't spook from this number. They'd come right in. But one season I got this harebrained idea to increase my spread to 9. Don't know why I decided to try this, but I did. And it sure as heck didn't work! Those ducks would flare from 9 almost every time. Had to go back to 7, then they started working again."

Howdy fellas! A mallard drake lights into a companionable group of decoys.

(To this day, I don't know if he was pulling the leg of his naive southern visitor or if he truly believed that black ducks had some natural predisposition to come to 7 decoys but not to 9.)

A few years later I was guiding on Lake Barkley in western Kentucky from a big open-water blind surrounded by 400 decoys, many of which were plastic milk jugs covered in black roofing pitch. I scattered these jugs randomly among my regular duck decoys. This spread looked quite unnatural to the human eye, but the ducks loved it.

In late winter, we always had several black ducks on the lake, and they worked this setup with little hesitation. Each time I retrieved a black duck from my ragtag decoys, I wondered what George Soule would say about my spread's attraction to his beloved ebony birds. I also questioned how effective my "decoys" would be on black ducks in the salt bays along the upper East Coast.

Through the decades, North American waterfowlers have devised many decoy strategies for luring ducks into close shotgun range. Inventive minds and trial-and-error testing have conjured up decoy systems specific to small ponds and marshes, large open lakes, coastal bays, flooded timber, dry fields, and other settings where these ducks and geese are hunted.

What follows are detailed descriptions of how fourteen of North America's most successful duck hunters set their decoys to lure birds into a diverse range of marsh, bay, lake, and land.

Jon Butler: Cypress Brakes, Standing-water Swamps

Jon Butler of Jackson, Tennessee, hunts in the Forked Deer River bottoms in a swamp that holds water year-round. Butler maintains permanent blinds on two open holes that are surrounded by cypress and tupelo trees, buck brush, saw grass, and other emergent vegetation. These holes measure approximately 80 X 110 yards and 90 X 120 yards respectively. Water depth averages 2 feet but will rise to 4 feet after a heavy rain.

Butler bags mostly puddle ducks from his blinds, but also works Canada geese into the larger hole. Through years of experimenting, he has devised what he feels is the most effective decoy spread for this site and situation.

"This is not a feeding area," Butler explains. "Instead, it's a rest area that waterfowl come to after feeding at night or early in the morning. We hunt from dawn to mid-afternoon, and our best hunting typically comes from 10 a.m. to 2 p.m., when big flights of birds are migrating or trading back and forth between local refuges. They fly down the bottoms in high formation, and by using large, visible decoy spreads and persuasive calling, we can break 'em out and pull 'em in. We routinely work flights of 25 to 100 ducks."

Decoys

Butler's blinds are built on stakes at the edge of open water, so he doesn't have the option of moving them to adjust for different winds. Thus he has devised a decoy spread that will work regardless of wind direction. "It's a split design, like a horseshoe," he says. "I set one big bunch of decoys off the left corner of each blind, running them out about 35 yards. Next I string a few decoys across the front of the blind, no farther than 15 yards out. Then I extend another bunch of decoys off the right corner. This provides a large, open landing hole right in front of the blind. This is where most ducks work regardless of wind direction."

Butler sets approximately 250 decoys in his larger hole and 200 in his smaller hole. All are oversized decoys for better visibility. "I'm a big believer in visibility," he says. "Those high flights have to be able to see a spread before they'll pitch to it."

He mainly uses mallard decoys, but also mixes in several black ducks, which show up better at long distances. He adds in a few pintails, coots, wigeon, and gadwall for extra realism. In the larger hole, he also sets out 3 dozen Canada goose floaters on the end of the right arm of the horseshoe.

Butler rigs a decoy jerk cord for each arm of each blind's spread to provide movement on days when the wind is calm. (He usually attaches four decoys per line.) Also, he sets out various motorized decoys for the same purpose. He says, "On no-wind days, having a lot of movement in the spread is critical to drawing birds in."

To top it off, Butler adds a few extra touches to enhance his spreads' attraction to passing waterfowl. In the small hole, an old beaver hut sits in the middle of the landing area, between the two arms of the spread. Butler has rounded the hut off and set a half-dozen standup (field) duck decoys on top of it for

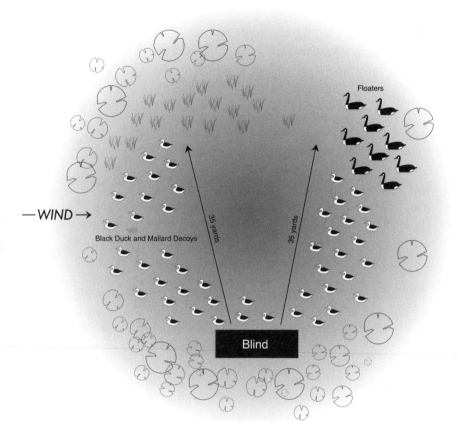

Floaters

—WIND→

Black Duck and Mallard Decoys

35 yards

35 yards

Blind

Butler's horseshoe pattern for cypress breaks and standing-water swamps deploys up to 250 oversized decoys to pull ducks into the open landing hole in front of the blind.

extra realism. "I like to study how real ducks sit on the water, and if there's a beaver hut or log or some similar object around, there are always a few ducks up there resting and preening," he says. "This is what I'm copying by putting those standup decoys up there." Butler also adds a great blue heron decoy at the edge of each hole for more realism.

Describing his spreads, he says: "In the type of spot where I hunt, you need a spread that can be seen a long way off, which you achieve with lots of big decoys. Next, the more natural-looking the spread is, the more effective it'll be. When ducks and geese get in there for a close inspection, I want my decoys to look as real as possible.

"Also, I think it's vital to leave a wide-open landing hole where a big flight of ducks can drop in. And the last thing doesn't have anything to do with decoys, but it's crucial to success. I camouflage my blinds with oak brush and vines that blend in with the natural vegetation around my holes. I really pile it on. I don't think you can have too much cover on your blind."

Rick Nemecek: Freshwater Marsh Spread

Rick Nemecek of Port Clinton, Ohio, is a lifelong duck hunter and longtime guide in the Sandusky Bay marshes on the south shore of Lake Erie. Nemecek's grandfather guided here in the early 1900s. Today Nemecek guides at the Winous Point Shooting Club, the oldest actively chartered duck club in North America (1856). He also hunts on local public shooting areas. A freelance outdoor writer and magazine editor in "real life," Nemecek abandons his desk when the waterfowl season opens and hunts every day.

The Sandusky Bay marshes are a maze of cattails, reeds, and open-water potholes that average 50 to 100 yards across. Before a hunt, Nemecek will scout to learn where puddle ducks are working, then set up in a promising spot. Sometimes he hunts from a fixed blind or a punt boat, but usually he huddles in natural cover as he attempts to toll birds in.

In so doing, Nemecek uses a small decoy spread, but one that is assembled through experience to draw birds. "I'll use 12 to 18 decoys in the early season, and I'll increase this number up to 3 dozen in the late season. Early-season ducks aren't as wary, and they fly low over the marsh. But later in the season the ducks are smarter, and they fly higher, so I feel I need more decoys to attract their attention."

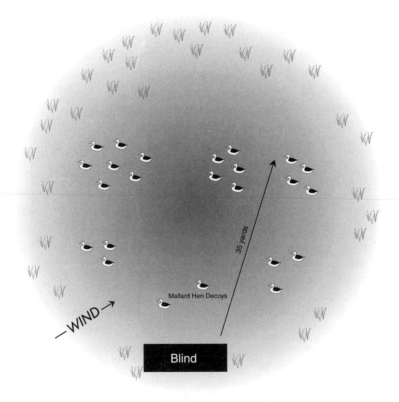

Freshwater marsh spread. Black or dark-colored decoys make this spread stand out to passing ducks, so Nemecek uses up to 3/4 black ducks in his spread.

Nemecek believes high visibility is a key to success in decoying ducks in the marsh, and he has a trick for making his small spreads stand out. "I'm a big believer in using black or dark-colored decoys," he confides. "Decoys have become almost photolike in their paint schemes, but hens, especially, are colored the way they are so they'll blend into their surroundings. This doesn't help when you're trying to draw ducks from long distance. Instead, you want decoys that'll catch their eye. Black decoys have a much greater color contrast than natural-colored decoys."

Putting out a few pintails can add greatly to your spread's visibility.

Nemecek continues, "I've talked to biologists who fly aerial waterfowl surveys, and they've told me the first thing they notice when they see ducks on the water is their black profiles. So my early-season spread will include ⅓ to ½ black duck decoys, and by the later season I'll increase this number up to ¾ black ducks. Then the next thing the biologists tell me they see is white, so I always set 2 to 3 pintail drakes in my spread.

Duck Spreads

"My typical early-season spread of 18 decoys includes 7 to 8 black ducks, 3 pintail drakes—and the rest mallards. In the later season, my spread of 36 decoys includes 24 black ducks, 3 pintails, and 9 mallards."

Nemecek likes magnum-size decoys—not super magnums, and not standards. He explains, "I can carry more magnum decoys than super magnums. Also, I feel that in a marsh, numbers are more important than extra-large size." He rigs his decoys with Tanglefree lines and weights and keeps them in a mesh bag for transporting.

He allows the ducks to dictate where he sets his spread. "If I get to my chosen hole before shooting time, and I flush ducks off the water, I'll set my decoys where they got up. They were there for a reason. They may not always be on the upwind side of the hole, but I don't try to out-guess 'em. I just put the decoys where the ducks were." If he doesn't flush ducks, he sets his decoys at the spot that provides the best cover for hunting with the wind at his back.

He doesn't believe in standard patterns like a J-hook or U. "I believe these patterns become familiar to ducks that see them day after day. Instead, I set my stool in small family clusters with 3 to 6 decoys per cluster. Now the overall pattern may be a J or a U, but it's loose. The clusters don't run together to form long strings."

Nemecek sets his most natural looking decoys closest to where he's hiding. "I think when ducks get in close, detail can make a difference. I feel they come to the best, most realistic decoys, and I want these right in front of my blind. I always like to have a hen mallard closest to my calling location."

He also sets several motion decoys in this area. In the past, he has used 3 to 4 wobblers or feeding decoys, but now he uses a half-dozen H_2O Magnets scattered throughout the close portion of his spread. These water shakers create a ripple on calm days that adds life to his spread.

Nemecek offers one other tip for hunting in marshes. "When I'm working ducks, I'll call 'em until it's time to shoot. I don't quit calling when they head in my direction. Now I may tone down the volume and change my cadence, but I still coax the ducks all the way to the water. I feel that too many hunters lose birds' attention when they quit calling."

Harry Boyle: Pinwheel Spread for Flooded Fields

Harry Boyle of Chico, California, is known as the King of Quack, and if you have a question about duck hunting, just ask him. If anything, Boyle is not shy about sharing his opinions on how to fool these birds into close shotgun range. He's learned many tricks in his thirty years of professional guiding and managing duck clubs in the Sacramento Valley.

Specifically, Boyle sinks pits and hunts over large decoy spreads in rice fields that are flooded an average of 8 inches deep. He mostly decoys puddle ducks: mallards, pintails, gadwall, wigeon, teal, and wood ducks. "My pits will shoot four hunters," he explains. "I bury these in rice levees right up to the very top of the pits, then I cover the openings with natural vegetation. I don't like to use rolling tops on my pits. When you roll the top back, it scares the ducks. Movement is the enemy of hunters."

Boyle surrounds his pits with up to 350 decoys — mallards, pintails, and teal. He prefers using decoys of one size (not standards mixed with magnums, etc.), and he likes solid-keel models for greater stability in high wind. He ties every decoy by its front end. "On open water, live ducks all float facing into the wind. I achieve this look by tying my anchor strings beneath the head of the decoys."

Boyle divides his decoys into two equal groups, half in front of the pit-levee and half behind. His spread design resembles an old-fashioned pinwheel. The purpose of this pattern is to draw landing ducks to an

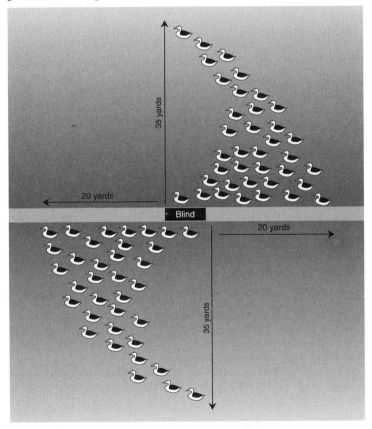

Pinwheel spread. Unique design draws ducks to an open hole in front of the pit under different wind conditions.

open hole in front of the pit regardless of wind direction. "Our prevailing winds are north and south, and this spread allows us to take advantage of either of these directions," Boyle explains. "Say the pit is on a levee running east and west. If the wind is from the north, hunters can shoot at ducks sailing upwind out of the south side of the pit. If the wind's from the south, they can shoot out of the north side of the pit. So this spread works on either wind."

Assume the wind is from the south, and hunters are facing the north (downwind). Boyle starts his spread by dropping decoys close to the left edge of the pit, then running them along the outside edge at an angle across and a few yards in front of the pit. Then Boyle hooks this outside line back to the left, stopping it 40 yards in front of the blind. (From inside the pit, this outer edge of the spread traces a reverse C.) From this point 40 yards out, Boyle runs the right edge of the spread back to the levee 20 yards to the right of the blind. Next he fills in between these two edges in a solid mat with decoys placed 2 feet apart.

He duplicates this spread on the opposite side of the levee to take advantage of a north wind. With hunters turned to face south, decoys on this side of the levee are set exactly the way they are on the north side. Thus, from overhead, the decoys would be set in a pinwheel design, one half of the spread a mirror image of the other. "North wind, south, east, west, northwest, southeast, whatever—ducks turning upwind always have an open landing area next to the main body of decoys directly in front of the blind. It works like a charm!" Boyle exclaims.

This guide isn't particular about each individual decoy's appearance, but he makes sure the white breasts on his pintail decoys are "bright white" with new paint each season. This white shows up a long way and is a natural color to live birds.

Beyond setting a good decoy spread, Boyle has other tips for hunting ducks in rice fields. "Hunters should either disk a rice field before flooding it, or they should 'stomp' it (wet rolling after the field is flooded). Either process turns the field into a gooey mess that the ducks love. It exposes roots and invertebrates they feed on. It's just a legal means of making a rice field far more attractive to ducks."

Also, when hunting over a rice field setup, Boyle advises hunters to call with braggadocio. "They should call loud, hard, and incessantly," he explains. "They should use highballs until the ducks are 200 yards out and working, then tone it down to three-note hurry-ups, mixing in some lonesome hen and resting chuckle calls. Then when they turn downwind, get on 'em again. If it's the right kind of day, I call 'em until it's time to shoot."

Boyle adds that bad calling is worse than no call-ing. "If you don't know how to blow a call, if you don't have the rhythm or sounds down pat, then leave the call in your pocket. Or blow a sprig whistle. It's hard to mess that one up."

Mel DeLang: River Chute Two-spread Set

Mel DeLang has seen many sunrises from duck blinds in southeast Iowa. DeLang, from Burlington, guided for forty years on the Mississippi River and the Lake Odessa wildlife area. He is also a former world champion duck caller (1963), and he has judged numerous duck calling contests, including three world championships.

Now in his late sixties, DeLang has given up guiding and competition calling, but he still hunts every day of the season from a permanent blind on a chute just off the Mississippi River, the former Lakewood Hunting Club. This is a typical open-water setup, where the decoys are exposed to strong winds and currents. DeLang and his partners maintain three blinds, each of which is complemented with its own large permanent spread of up to 300 decoys.

"We use this many decoys for greater visibility and attraction to high passing ducks," DeLang explains. "We use all super magnums, mostly mallards with a few pintails mixed in. Mallards are the main ducks we're hunting. Also, we set about 50 Canada goose floaters off to one side of the blind and another 75 standup fullbody geese on a mud flat behind our main blind."

The river slough where DeLang hunts is approximately two miles long by 200 yards wide. It is totally open—no brush or trees. It is also shallow, 2½ feet deep when the Mississippi River is at pool stage at Burlington. "The chute runs north and south, and our blind is just out in the water off the west bank," says DeLang.

DeLang hunts over what he describes as a "two-spread setup." Basically, this is a separate, rounded decoy spread of equal size off each corner of the blind with an open "meat hole" in the middle. Decoys in each spread are concentrated within 45 yards of the blind. The goose floaters are set off the north back corner of the blind, between the ducks and the mud flat. Then the standup geese are spread behind the blind on the mud.

"Our best winds for working ducks are northwest, west, and southwest, and with this setup they'll hook around and land in the open hole between the two spreads," DeLang explains. He adds that this setup doesn't work as well on an east wind, but the breeze blows rarely from this direction in southeast Iowa.

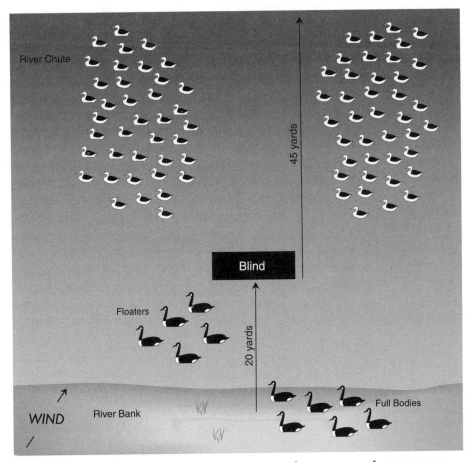

River chute set. A large permanent open-water setup with two groups of super magnum mallards tolls passing ducks into the "meat hole" in the middle. Note the Canada goose floaters off to one side and the full-body standup geese on the mudflat behind the blind.

DeLang ties his decoys with heavy parachute cord and anchors them individually with home-poured concrete anchors "the size of a Styrofoam beer cup." He says the heavy weights are necessary for days when the wind or river currents kick up.

"I like to set each decoy individually instead of running them on long lines the way some open-water hunters do," DeLang continues. "I think the random spread looks more natural. I cut my anchor lines 4 feet long (again, for 2½ feet of water), and I set my decoys 2 feet apart. This way, when the wind changes, all the decoys can swing together without tangling."

Two major problems with this type spread are ice and rising water. "When ice begins forming, we start pulling decoys," DeLang says. "If it gets really icy, we'll pick up all the decoys, then put out what we want to hunt over each day. If we leave 'em out, ice floes will carry them down the river."

DeLang does likewise when the water level begins rising. "When the water comes up, logs and debris will snag our decoys and scatter them from here to St. Louis. So we keep a careful watch during a rise, and we pick up the decoys if we have to."

DeLang has a system for quick decoy pickup. "I attach a snap swivel to each anchor, and when I pick up a decoy, I just unsnap the weight and then put the decoy in the pile without winding up the cord. Those heavy parachute cords won't tangle. This system is faster than wrapping the anchor and string around each decoy."

One thing DeLang is fastidious about in his open-water spread is keeping decoys untangled. "I hate the sound of decoys bumping together. With the way we rig our set, we usually don't get many tangles unless there's a big blow. But when tangles happen, I straighten them out. Tangles might not bother the ducks as much as they bother me, but I don't tolerate 'em!"

Wade Bourne: Open-lake Doughnut Hole Spread

Let me get personal here. For several years back in the late 1970s and early '80s, my hunting partners

Phil Sumner and Don Buck and I maintained a large floating blind on Lake Barkley in western Kentucky. This blind was anchored on an open flat in 6-foot water beneath a flyway that ducks and geese followed up and down the reservoir. It was not a natural feeding or rafting spot, but through sheer decoy and calling power, we were able to break passing flights down and work them in.

Through the seasons, we devised what we called our "doughnut hole spread." In essence, we set decoys completely around the blind in a ring that extended out to 40 yards. The blind floated in a hole in the middle of the spread, and the blind was moored so that it would swing with the wind and always face downwind. Thus regardless of wind direction, when we came up to shoot, the birds were always coming head-on.

We engineered this by bolting a steel cable to each back corner of the blind. Then these two cables were coupled together 6 feet behind the blind to form a Y. From this point, a single cable extended down to the anchor point in the water (two old car engine blocks chained together). Thus rigged, the blind became a large wind vane that pivoted freely around the anchor, in the center of the "doughnut hole." The innermost decoys in the spread were set just outside the radius of swing.

As mentioned in this chapter's introduction, we used approximately 400 decoys in this set, ⅔ ducks and ⅓ one-gallon milk jugs that had been dipped in a roofing pitch-gasoline mixture to coat them flat black. These black jugs added greatly to the spread's visibility over long distances, plus they danced back and forth in the slightest breeze. The ducks loved them.

For rigging, we used 8-foot lengths of salvaged electrical wire. Our anchors were whole bricks. The wire wouldn't wear through by rubbing against the bricks' rough edges.

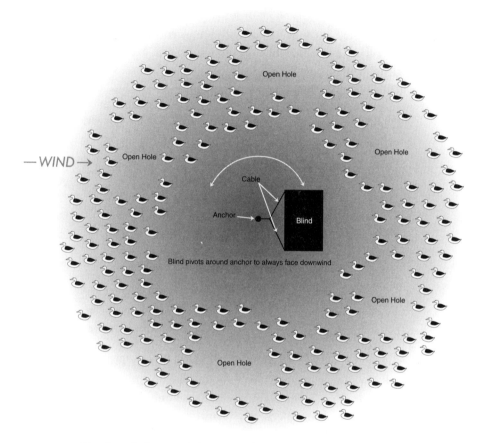

Doughnut hole spread. A pivoting floating blind in the center hole allows hunters head-on shots regardless of wind direction. Smaller open holes throughout the spread provide landing zones for incoming ducks.

We set our decoys with thinned-out holes so that the ducks could alight inside the spread. Sometimes they'd try to land on the outside edge, but by bearing down with a call, we could usually pull them a few yards closer.

Setting this doughnut hole spread took at least one full day of rigging and another day to transport and place the decoys. However, we left the spread out for the duration of the season. Our enemies were ice, storm winds, and sudden water rises. Any of these conditions would require quick attention to the spread to rescue decoys that were being blown or dragged away, and to undo tangles.

This spread required a lot of work to rig and maintain, but the results were worth the effort. When big migrating flights of mallards rolled down the lake, they found our spread and highball style of calling hard to resist. We enjoyed many great hunts there, and still share wonderful memories of the days spent overlooking our doughnut hole rig.

George Cochran: Decoys in Flooded Timber

George Cochran of Hot Springs, Arkansas, is famous in the outdoor sporting world—for bass fishing. Cochran is a two-time winner of the Bass Masters Classic. He has also won several other national fishing titles. However, when duck season opens in Arkansas, look for Cochran in the flooded green timber. He has prowled this state's public management areas for more than thirty years. He hunts virtually every day of the season. For George Cochran, bass fishing is his living; duck hunting in flooded timber is his passion.

Cochran says bass fishing and duck hunting in timber are similar in one respect. "On any given reservoir, most fish will be concentrated in small areas. The same is true of ducks. One of the big management areas I hunt spans 36,000 acres, but the ducks usually gang up in 10 to 15 percent of this area. They move around a lot as water and weather conditions change. So scouting is critical. To have a good hunt, you've got to be where the ducks are."

Cochran continues, "Now when hunting pressure is heavy, which it typically is where I hunt, the ducks

Decoys

Decoys placed around the edges of a hole in flooded timber will look more natural to passing ducks than those placed in the middle.

like to work into thick brush more than open woods. And they're really wary because there's so much calling and shooting throughout the woods. They get educated pretty fast. After opening week, it's rare for 'em to fly around a hole a time or two and then fall in like they used to in the old days. Back then we just hid behind trees and called and kicked the water, and that was enough attraction for 'em. But today they circle and circle, and they want to see some ducks on the water before they'll come in. So now we put out decoys every day we hunt."

Specifically, Cochran and his buddies set spreads of 15 to 75 decoys, depending on the size of their hole and how difficult it is to reach. They boat in as close as they can, then wade where the boats won't go. As they wade, they float or carry their decoys in mesh bags, then scatter them around small, natural openings in the timber, usually where a tree has fallen over.

"The way you set the decoys is extremely important," Cochran stresses. "Most hunters want to set their

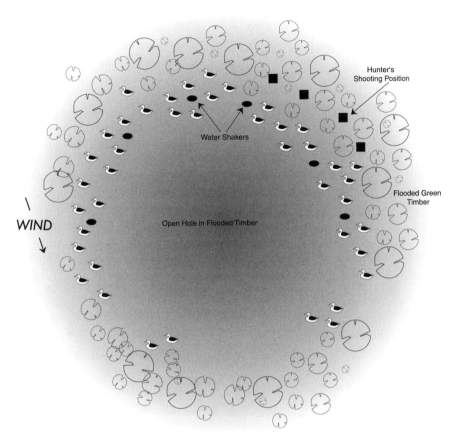

Flooded timber spread. Apart from decoy placement, movement is key to this setup's success. Thus Cochran uses up to 8 shaker decoys and his "convincer" jerk string for plenty of motion.

decoys right in the middle of their hole, but we've learned it's better to drop them around the edges of the hole, leaving the middle open. This looks like ducks have landed, and they're swimming out into the timber. It's more natural, and with decoys set around the sides, circling ducks can see decoys whether they're on the upwind or downwind side of the hole."

Decoys

Something else they do is add movement to their spread with shaker decoys and sometimes an elastic jerk string with a couple of decoys tied on it. "The shakers are battery-operated. We'll put out up to 8 shakers, setting one every few yards around the perimeter of the hole. They can make the difference between success and failure on calm-wind days.

"But the jerk string is what really fires 'em up. We call it our 'convincer.' We rig it with a long bungee cord and a string with a hen and drake decoy tied on. The bungee cord is tied to a tree or heavy weight at one end. Then the string is stretched back across the hole. When ducks are circling in close, we'll let the string go, and the constricting bungee cord will ski the two decoys across the hole like the drake's chasing the hen, trying to mate with her. Usually, when circling ducks see this, they'll ball up and fall right in." (See chapter 5 for complete details on rigging the "convincer" jerk string.)

Cochran isn't particular about what type and size decoys he uses in flooded timber. "We use several different sizes and shapes; it doesn't seem to matter. But what does matter is movement! That's what the ducks spot, what they like." Cochran rigs his decoys with 3-foot strings and 6-ounce trotline weights.

"We've learned one other thing that's really important for hunting in the late season," he adds. "When the ducks are extremely wary, they'll work into little bitty openings in the thickest, brushiest woods in the area. These are places where we won't use more than 15 decoys plus our shakers."

Overcalling is a sure way to spook 'em, says Cochran. "When they're skittish, I'll make one short highball on their first pass, then I'll shut up and let 'em work on their own. Once I tell 'em I'm there, I don't call anymore. I think the biggest mistake hunters make in flooded timber, especially from Christmas on, is calling too much."

Jim Reid: Freelance Duck Spreads

Forget the permanent blinds and mega-decoy spreads. Jim Reid of Wichita, Kansas, is a freelance hunter. He shifts from this state's reservoirs to marshes to rivers as weather conditions change and concentrations of ducks move about. Reid has hunted from boats and temporary shore blinds for more than thirty years. During this time he has perfected a decoy system that is both versatile and deadly.

"I go where the ducks are," Reid affirms. "I scout a lot of afternoons to see where they're resting and feeding. Typically I'll set up in a loafing area and catch 'em coming back from the fields in mid-morning. This might be on a reservoir point, on a flat in the head of a reservoir, on a marsh, or on a river sandbar. The ducks move frequently, so being mobile is the key to staying in the action."

On big water, Reid hunts from a 16-foot johnboat fitted with a Go-Devil motor and an Avery portable boat-blind. In marshes, he may switch to a canoe to paddle into hard-to-reach holes. And when river hunting, he usually walks to selected sites from the closest road.

One of Reid's favorite setups is on a point of land jutting out into a reservoir. "If the wind's not too strong, mallards and other puddlers like to loaf around these points. I'll hunt such a spot either from land or from my boat blind if there's any cover to hide the boat in."

Reid's reservoir spread consists of 60 duck decoys, half magnums and half super magnums. He uses all mallards except for 6 super magnum pintail drakes. "The white color on the pintails shows up well, and I think the ducks like that," Reid notes.

He also sets out 6 to 10 Canada goose floaters. "I use these as much to attract ducks as I do geese," Reid explains. "We're talking visibility. The goose decoys are big, and ducks can see 'em farther. It's surprising how often ducks will land with the geese instead of with the duck decoys."

Reid rigs his decoys with 7-foot strings and 8-ounce wrap-around strap weights for the ducks and 16-ounce weights for the geese. He keeps his decoys bagged for backpacking or transporting in his boat.

"If I can, I like to set up on a point with the sun behind me and the wind coming from either the left or right," Reid says. "I'll set a decoy spread that's similar to a check mark or the old fisherman's hook. I'll start out with a long downwind string, then curl my decoys around upwind, leaving a nice open pocket in front of the blind. This spread is sort of like a curving teardrop with the sharp point downwind."

Specifically, Reid begins his line approximately 50 yards downwind. Here decoys will be set sparsely, 6 to 8 feet apart for some 10 yards. Then as he works toward the blind, he begins thickening the line and setting decoys closer together. Finally, as he makes his curl on the upwind side of the blind, he groups his decoys with no semblance of a line.

The goose decoys go on the upwind side of the spread, just beyond the ducks. Also, Reid sets 3 "lander" duck decoys (2 hens and a drake) in the opening where he wants real ducks to settle.

"When ducks come into this set, they'll sail up the line to the open area next to the group, into the curve of the hook," Reed attests. "A lot of times they'll home in on the landers and drop in right beside them."

Duck Spreads

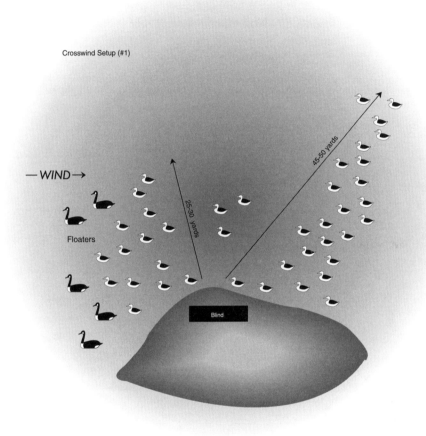

Crosswind reservoir setup. This fishhook pattern calls for 60 duck decoys (half magnums and half super magnums) and up to 10 Canada goose floaters for added visibility.

Sometimes Reid modifies this rig according to wind conditions. "If the wind is coming off my back, I'll change the spread from a fishhook to a nice wide V. Also, if it's a windless day, which we rarely have in

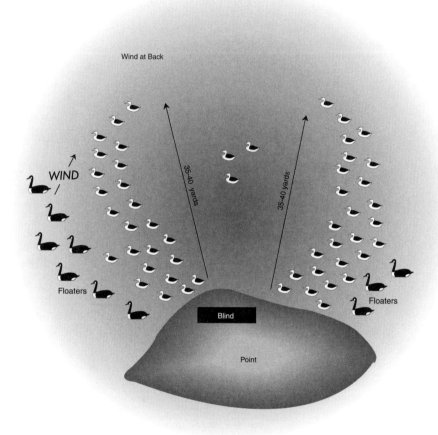

Reid modifies his reservoir spread from a fishhook to a wide V when the wind is at his back.

Kansas, I'll rig 2 or 3 decoys on a jerk string (stake and bungee cord) to provide some movement."

If there is too much wind—blowing thirty to forty miles per hour—Reid shifts his spread to the lee side of the point. "The ducks won't land out where the waves are breaking, so I move around to the sheltered side of the point. This is just a matter of watching where the birds want to be."

Later in the season, when ponds and shallow marshes begin freezing over, many ducks relocate to Kansas's wide, shallow rivers. They continue to feed in dry fields in the morning, then spend midday snoozing and collecting grit on river sandbars. "I use a lot of shell decoys when hunting the sandbars, since I can carry several dozen in a bag. Two hunters can easily carry more than a hundred shells without too much problem." Reid also uses several floater decoys and 8 to 10 Canada goose shells on the rivers. "I feel that the more decoys you can set out on a sandbar, the better off you are," Reid notes. "Live birds gather in big concentrations on the rivers, so a big decoy spread is very natural."

Reid usually looks for a stretch of river that runs east and west, then selects a sandbar within shooting range of the upwind bank and builds a natural cover blind. Next he begins setting a "resting spread" of shell decoys. "If the wind's not too high, we just pop the heads on and drop the shells onto the sand. We'll turn some of the heads backwards like the ducks are sleeping or preening, and we'll rig others like they're eating some grit. We'll make two or three different groupings on the sand, leaving some open landing areas in front of the blind."

Reid drops his floating decoys in the shallow water adjacent to the sandbar where they will swim in the current. He also stakes more shells into the shallows immediately adjacent to the sand, like the ducks are walking up onto the sandbar. Finally, he places his goose decoys on one end of the spread.

"You can manipulate this spread however you need to relative to the wind and your water-sandbar

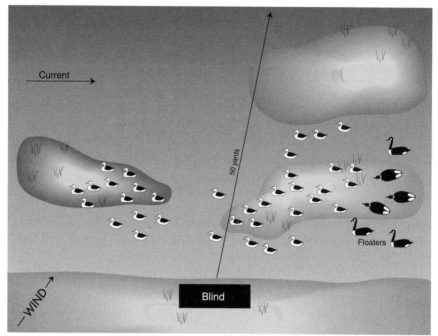

Reid's late-season river spread. Shell decoys placed on the sandbars imitate ducks that are sleeping and collecting sand grit.

configuration. Incoming ducks will usually land in the water. I think the important thing is to leave a good open landing area in the shallows close to the mass of your spread. If you do this properly, you can work some big flights of ducks right to your shotgun bead."

Don Jensen: Decoying Field-feeding Ducks

In fall in southern Alberta, mallards and pintails swarm barley and pea fields like locusts, descending in huge flocks to gorge on these delectable crops. In so doing, they offer hunters some unique challenges: how to hide in broad, open fields; how to decoy large groups of birds; how to call to a thousand ducks at once.

Don Jensen runs a guide-outfitter business called Wildlife West Adventures, Inc., and he's figured these problems out. Jensen's hunters routinely take 8-duck limits over field spreads, sometimes so quickly that the hunt is over almost before it starts. "When everything clicks, field shooting can be fast and furious," Jensen says. "For instance, recently I guided six hunters who took 48 mallards and pintails in eighteen minutes. Now it's obviously not always this fast, but field shooting can be very, very exciting."

Jensen says that "spotting" is the first key to success in field shooting. "You've got to do your homework. You've got to pinpoint and set your spread on the exact spot the ducks are working, not just close by. Being off by 200 yards can keep you from having a good hunt."

Most days, ducks feed in dry fields in early morning and late afternoon. Jensen scouts the afternoon before a morning hunt or the morning (same day) before an afternoon hunt. He gets an exact fix on where ducks are feeding, and this is where he sets his decoys when he returns. "Typically we'll hunt in a barley field that's swathed (grain cut and raked into rows for ripening). These rows average 15 yards apart. I'll set two Final Approach Eliminator (layout) blinds side by side in three parallel rows (six blinds total), all facing downwind.

"Next I'll set out 5 to 6 dozen Canada goose shells, starting around the blinds and stretching 20 yards downwind on the swathed rows. I may put a decoy or two between the rows, but most of the decoys will actually be on the windrowed grain.

"And last I'll toss out 500 to 1,000 pieces of light-weight black roofing paper, starting at the edge of the geese and scattering them downwind along the

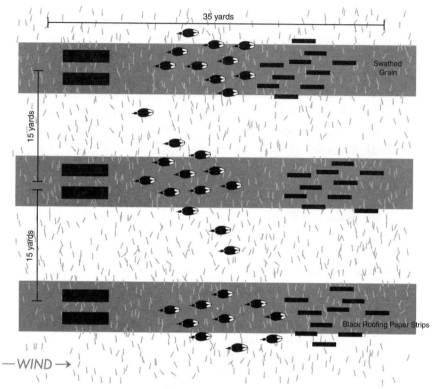

Field spread for ducks. The blinds, Canada goose shells, and black roofing paper are placed directly on the windrows of barley to simulate feeding ducks and geese.

windrows for another 15 yards. So the distance from the upwind edge of the spread to the downwind edge is approximately 35 yards—good shooting range."

Jensen uses the lightest, cheapest roofing paper he can buy. "You want lightweight paper so it'll wave in the wind," he explains. "The paper I use is about the same weight as typing paper." He tears this paper into "decoys" that are 4 to 6 inches wide by 10 to 12 inches long. He transports these tarpaper strips in a large bag.

"One hunter can put these 'decoys' out in just a few minutes," Jensen explains. "You don't place them by hand. Instead, you just walk along and deal them like playing cards, letting them fall into the stubble. Or you might toss out 20 at a time and kick the piles to scatter them. Some will lie flat; others will lie on their edges. It doesn't matter. The idea is to blacken the windrows with those tarpaper strips. Don't worry about where they fall or how they look. Just put 'em out there, climb into your blinds, and get ready to shoot."

Jensen says the best days for hunting ducks in dry fields are windy and overcast, perhaps with a light snow or fog. A poor day is one with no wind and a bright sky. If the wind is blowing thirty miles per hour or harder, the ducks may fly all day or will fly earlier in the afternoon. He recommends setting up by 1 p.m. for an afternoon hunt on a gusty day.

Jensen says that the tarpaper decoys don't work well in rain, since the paper shines. They are good in snow, however. He simply sets the goose decoys and tarpaper strips on top of the snow, dons white camouflage, and hunts as usual.

Jensen feels that calling can spook ducks working a field set. "My rule is not to call when they're coming," he says. "I might do some soft chuckling or blow a sprig whistle a little bit, but I won't do any highballing."

One other scenario he encounters infrequently is hunting in a harvested pea field where there is no windrowed grain. "Ducks absolutely love peas," Jensen notes. "When we hunt a pea field, we set up in the exact spot where the birds were the last time they fed, and we make a black streak across the field. We'll scatter the paper strips first. We'll just take an armful and toss them up into the wind and kick them with our feet. Then we'll set the goose decoys and blinds up-wind from the paper strips. We'll use the goose shells to help hide the blinds."

Jensen adds that when ducks are hunted in a field, they will normally abandon it for at least a couple of days. "Ducks in fields are very sensitive to hunting pressure. So I scout constantly and try to have several fields available. I'll hunt one one day and another the next. You can't hunt the same field two days in a row and expect the second hunt to be any good."

Mark Burch: Decoy Spreads for Ice

When ice forms on a lake or marsh, ducks shift to areas where they can still find open water. This may be bigger lakes in the same vicinity or farther down the flyway. They don't all leave at once, however. And after a hard freeze hits, hunters may still have a few good days of shooting if they know how to set a decoy spread in or on ice.

Mark Burch of Humansville, Missouri, does this frequently in the late season. Burch guides for ducks and geese (mainly mallards and Canadas) on nearby Truman Reservoir. He hunts from permanent bank blinds next to shallow flats. When a freeze arrives, he continues to hunt these spots as long as birds are present, and he alters his decoy spread according to the severity of the freeze and, specifically, the thick-ness of the ice.

"The first day or two after a freeze hits, I'll keep a hole of open water broken out in front of the blind," Burch says. "I'll bust a half-moon-shaped hole some 50 yards out from the blind. I'll do this with a small boat, pushing and rocking it to break the ice up so the wind will blow it to the downwind side of the hole. Or if there's no wind blowing, I'll break off large sheets and float them under the unbroken ice around the edge of the hole. In either case, the idea is to open up a hole that's big enough for passing ducks and geese to see at long distances."

Next Burch sets 2 to 3 dozen duck decoys in the hole in a J formation with the long arm extending downwind. "One thing I do in an ice hole is pack my decoys in closer to the blind. When it's extremely cold, ducks are less wary, and it's easier to get them to commit to the decoys. The closer they're landing, the better the shooting will be."

Burch then sets several dozen Canada goose decoys (shells and full-bodies) on the side and upwind edge of the hole, actually sitting on the ice next to the open water. He faces these into the wind, and he creates two or more family groupings for realism's sake. He explains, "It's common for ducks and geese to use the same open hole when ice starts forming. Now I'm hunting for geese too, but I'd still use the goose decoys if only the duck season was open. The goose decoys are big and dark, and they show up so well on the ice. They'll pull ducks from a long distance."

©Bill Buckley

If the freeze persists, keeping an open hole eventually becomes impossible, so Burch changes his decoy tactics. "In this case I'll go to an all–Canada goose spread and put out as many Canada decoys as I can muster, usually around 300. If the shore is frozen hard, I can load my decoys on a trailer and drive them right to the blind. Then I'll walk the decoys onto the ice and set them out by hand.

Decoys

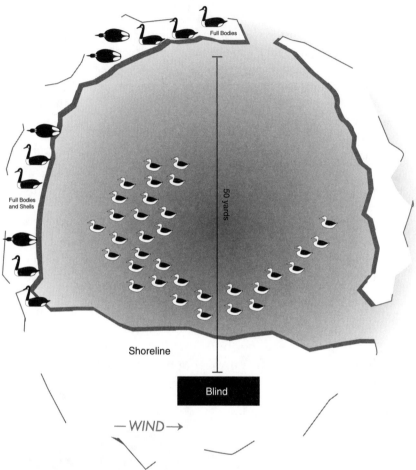

Ice spread. In a crosswind, break a 50-yard hole in the ice and set 2 to 3 dozen duck decoys in a J pattern and several dozen Canada goose decoys on the side and upwind edge of the hole.

It doesn't take too long to set the full spread this way, and mallards will work right into this all-goose setup."

If the wind is blowing from the blind's back, Burch will arrange his goose decoys in a U pattern with the upwind edge of the U just a few yards from the blind. If a crosswind is blowing, Burch simply makes

Duck Spreads

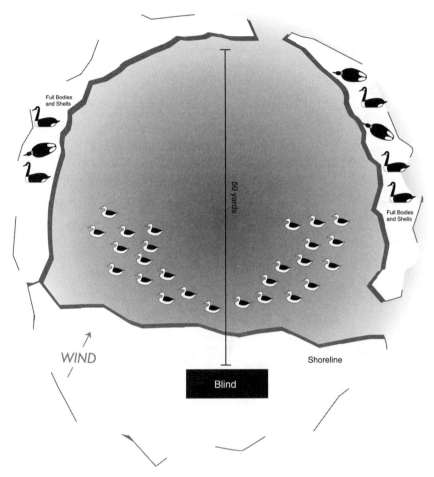

With the wind from the back, set the duck decoys in a U pattern and the goose decoys on both sides of the hole.

a "streak" of decoys in front of the blind running parallel to the wind's direction. He will arrange the "streak" so that the downwind edge is in front of the blind. This is where ducks will usually land.

"After a freeze, these spreads will give you a few more days of shooting, and they can be the best of the

Decoys

Frozen Pond

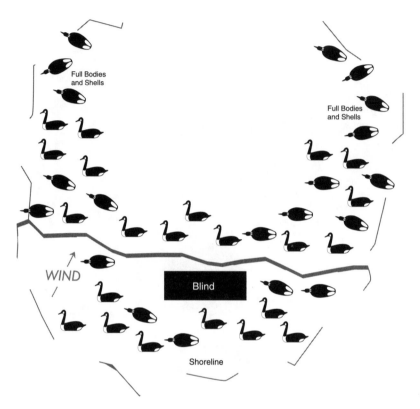

When keeping an open hole becomes impossible, use an all-Canada goose spread of up to 300 decoys, placed on the ice in a U pattern when the wind is at your back.

year," Burch says. "Ducks get real anxious for company when their resting areas start locking up. Usually they'll feed in dry fields at dawn and return to the lake by mid-morning. And suddenly they see this hole of water, if you have one, and this big concentration of birds, and as often as not they'll hook right in, many times without circling. This is when the shooting can be as good as it gets."

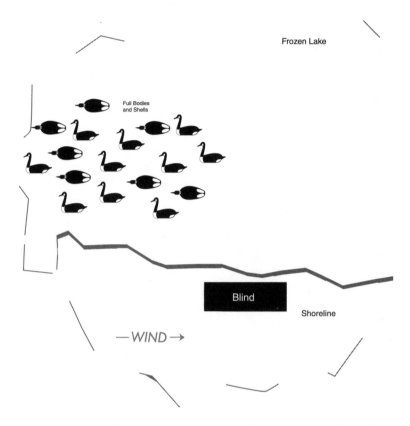

In a crosswind, place the goose decoys in a line running parallel to the wind's direction.

Tony Toye: Mixed Rig for Big-water Divers and Puddlers

Tony Toye of Boscobel, Wisconsin, operates Big River Guide Service on Pool 9 on the nearby Mississippi River. This pool is a major stopover area for migrating canvasbacks. Each year in October and early November, up to 300,000 cans gather here to feed on wild celery, fingernail clams, and zebra mussels along the pool's shallow shoreline areas. They stay until freeze-up pushes them on south.

And they have plenty company from other ducks. Redheads, mallards, wigeon, and various divers and puddlers also collect on Pool 9. This is a public shooting area, and Toye and others who hunt here routinely take their one allowable canvasback and a mixed bag of other birds. "Last year my parties took a total of 20 different species," Toye says. "We even shot a few sea ducks."

Thus Toye must set a decoy spread to draw both divers and puddlers. Also, since he's hunting adjacent to big, open water, his spread must be highly visible to flights of ducks trading at a distance.

"Permanent blinds aren't allowed on Pool 9, so I hunt from a 20-foot boat-blind rig that's covered in marsh grass to match the natural cover along the pool's shoreline," Toye continues. "I'll move around from day to day, setting up on islands, points, or feeding areas next to shore where ducks are flying back and forth. I'll anchor my boat next to the marsh grass, then I'll wade out and set my decoys by hand. The average water depth where I hunt is 2 to 4 feet."

Toye believes a big decoy spread is a must to draw the attention of passing birds. His normal set consists of 150 magnum decoys, half canvasbacks and half mallards. Also, he uses only drake canvasback decoys (no hens), and his drake-to-hen ratio with the mallard decoys is five to one. He explains, "In a flock of live birds, you have more drakes than hens, plus the drakes are more colorful. Ducks at long distance can see drakes better than they can hens, so I've just gone to using almost all drakes. I've never noticed any reluctance from live birds to work such a spread."

Each morning, Toye sets either of two basic spread designs, depending on wind direction. If the wind is directly at his back, he sets spread A. If he's setting up for a crosswind, he opts for spread B.

With spread A, he arranges a big "blob" of decoys on each side of the boat. "I'll start with about 60 canvasbacks on the side of the boat next to the open water. I'll spread these decoys 5 to 6 feet apart. Then I'll leave a small open space in front and set about 60 mallard decoys off the other corner of the boat. I'll drop the mallards closer together (2 to 3 feet apart), and I'll pack them in close to the boat. I want both blobs to look like large concentrations of feeding ducks."

Beyond these two "blobs," Toye leaves an open landing zone approximately 15 to 20 yards wide. Then beyond the landing zone, he strings out a smaller group of canvasbacks in front of the big concentration of cans and a smaller group of mallards in front of the large feeding group. Outside edges of these smaller groups are 40 to 50 yards from the boat blind. Decoys in both of these smaller groupings are spaced approximately 8 to 10 feet apart, and there is a wide gap between the two small groups.

"Here's the idea," Toye explains. "The big blobs of canvasbacks and mallards in close to the blind simulate feeding groups, and the smaller groupings out beyond the opening simulate smaller flocks that have landed and are swimming in to join the feeding groups.

"Now ducks are greedy birds by nature, and when a flock comes along and sees a smaller flight swimming into a larger one, they'll fly over the swimmers and land next to the feeding group to beat the swimmers to the food. The canvasbacks will land between the canvasback groups, and the mallards will land between the mallard groups. They'll do this every time."

Spread B applies the same logic, but the spread design is different to accommodate the crosswind.

Decoys

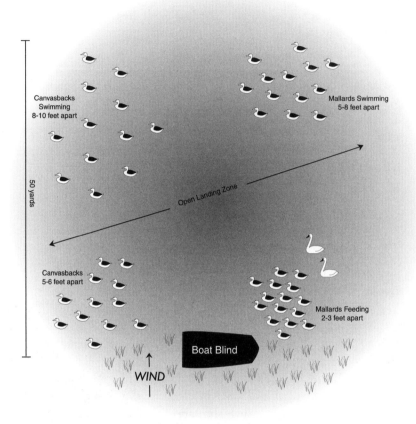

Big-water divers and puddlers, spread A. The smaller groups of decoys in the distance will simulate smaller flocks that are swimming to join the feeding groups near the blind. Ducks will fly over the swimmers and land next to the feeding group to beat the swimmers to the food.

In spread B, large (feeding) decoy concentrations of both canvasbacks and mallards are set on the upwind side of the boat blind. The mallard decoys are packed in close to the boat, and the canvasbacks are set farther out. An open zone some 5 feet wide separates the two large spreads. And again, the mallards are set 2 to 3 feet apart, the canvasbacks 5 to 6 feet apart.

An open landing zone 20 yards across is left in front of the boat. Then small swimmer groups of mallards and canvasbacks are set on the downwind side of the boat blind.

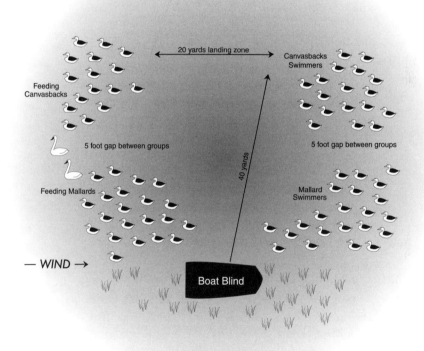

Spread B. In a crosswind the feeding groups are placed upwind from the swimmers and the effect is the same—passing ducks will land between the groups to beat the swimmers to the food.

The same principle applies in spread B as in spread A. Approaching ducks will circle downwind, then turn upwind and overfly the swimmer groups of decoys to land in the open area between the swimmer and feeder groups.

One added touch in Toye's spreads is the addition of two swan decoys on the outside edge of the group of feeding mallards. "We're seeing more and more swans in this area, so they're something of a confidence decoy for me. Also, my customers enjoy viewing swans, and when I can decoy some in, it's an extra treat for them."

Toye often hunts in choppy water and strong currents, so he rigs his decoys with long strings (8 feet) and 8-ounce wrap-around lead weights so that they will hold position.

He adds that proper calling plays a big role in getting ducks to commit to his decoys. "I power call to the mallards, with a lot of hail calls and loud persuasion. With the canvasbacks, it's just the opposite. I call very sparingly with them. I make a few purring sounds, but no highballing. They'll come by themselves if you'll just let them."

Larry Davis: Big-water Layout Boat Spreads

From his back porch, Larry Davis of Marblehead, Ohio, can throw a rock into Lake Erie. For forty-four years, Davis has made his living on this big water as a charter boat captain, commercial fisherman, and duck guide. In this latter endeavor, he has more than fifty years' experience in one of waterfowling's most unique, most exciting types of hunting—layout gunning. "This is the ultimate way to shoot ducks," Davis says. "In a layout boat, you're eyeball to eyeball with the birds. You can actually see the expressions on their faces."

Duck Spreads

Specifically, layout gunning involves setting a spread of diving duck decoys in open water, then anchoring low-profile gunning boats where hunters can shoot at incoming birds. The hunters recline and keep still as greater and lesser scaup (bluebills), canvasbacks, redheads, and other divers toll in. Then, when the ducks are in range, the hunters rise and fire.

"Lake Erie is a major stopover for diving ducks each fall," Davis explains. "They feed on aquatic grasses that grow up from the lake bottom. They gather in big rafts, sometimes thousands together. I scout these birds daily, and I learn their feeding areas and their flyways. I'll set my layout spread on a flyway between two rafts to lure ducks trading back and forth. I typically set up within ¾ mile of a major feeding area in water 3 to 20 feet deep."

Davis operates from a 38-foot tender boat, which carries two 14-foot one-man layout boats. He also tows an 18-foot V-hull with an outboard for setting out the spread and ferrying hunters to and from the layout boats.

According to Davis, the key to successful layout hunting is using a large number of decoys and arranging them properly. "I put out 82 bluebill decoys and 24 canvasbacks. I use hard foam decoys (Restle brand). If you shoot 'em, it doesn't hurt 'em. Also, these decoys are oversized, which adds to their visibility on open water." Davis rigs his decoys with forty-eight-thread green nylon twine and 1-pound lead mushroom anchors. He sets his spread in a horseshoe pattern with the open end of the horseshoe facing downwind. He groups his canvasback decoys together in the left arm of the horseshoe. "The spread will measure approximately 70 yards wide by 40 yards deep," he says. "Also, I don't like my decoys close together. I spread 'em 5 to 10 feet apart."

Davis anchors his two layout boats at the head of the horseshoe, just behind the upwind edge of the decoys. He positions the two boats a few feet apart, cocking them slightly to the right for right-shoulder shooters (more room to swing), and slightly left for left-shoulder shooters. "One thing is very important," Davis emphasizes. "You must leave open holes in the spread for ducks to land. Sometimes they'll hit the open part of the horseshoe, but more often they'll work right into the middle of the spread, to the holes. This is one of the main secrets for up-close shooting."

Davis usually leaves three to four open holes in his spread, with each hole measuring 30 to 40 feet in diameter. He makes sure these holes are within 20 yards of the layout boats for close shots. "I leave a hole in front of each boat and maybe another hole in each arm of the horseshoe," he explains.

When the spread is out, Davis transfers his hunters into the layout boats, then he runs the 18-foot boat back to the tender, anchored a half-mile away. From this point he watches the action through binoculars.

Davis says sometimes it's necessary to alter his spread to suit the ducks' whims. "I'll usually start out with the horseshoe set, but if they're landing on the edge or veering off, I'll make adjustments to the spread as necessary. Sometimes I'll close up the open end of the horseshoe and let the ducks work to the open holes. Other times I'll rearrange the spread in the shape of a fishhook. I'll do whatever it takes to pull 'em in for my hunters."

Davis says his favorite weather for layout shooting is a sunny day with a fifteen-mile-per-hour wind. "I don't like rain. The ducks don't decoy as well," he says.

He says singles and pairs generally decoy better than large flights of diving ducks. Also, he knows from experience that patience is a key to success in this game.

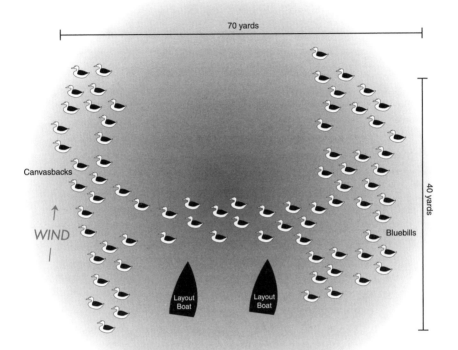

Layout boat spread. Ducks will work into the small open holes in the pattern more than into the open end of the horseshoe.

"Layout rigs don't always offer fast shooting. Sometimes it takes all day to bag limits."

Likewise, it takes a lot of time and effort to set and maintain a layout rig. "I can pick up a spread in around a half-hour; it takes less time to set it out. But all the work is worth it when the bluebills are buzzing around. This is truly an exciting way to hunt, one where the birds get right in your face."

Greg Karnes: Shoreline Sets for Diving Ducks

Greg Karnes is a partner in a hunting operation called Sportsman's Lodge in Sifton, Manitoba, west of gigantic Lakes Manitoba and Winnipegosis. From a waterfowler's perspective, this region has it all—big water and small potholes, and clouds of puddle ducks and divers. Karnes' guides lead his guests to a variety of shooting, but the lodge's specialty is gunning canvasbacks and redheads over decoys set along windswept shorelines bordering open water.

"I always hunt the downwind side of the lake," Karnes says. "I know most hunters believe you should hunt the upwind, calm side of the lake. But ducks in sheltered water don't stir around much; they just stay put, whereas ducks fly better where the water's rougher. So I go where the waves are rolling. They offer better shooting than flat-water areas."

Karnes, however, doesn't drop his decoys in the throat of a stout blow. Instead, he starts where the water is rough, then looks for some little break—a curved-in shoreline, the lee side of a point, or some

other lakeshore feature—that offers a pocket or sliver of water that's calmer than adjacent areas directly in the wind. "This is the key," Karnes says. "A flight of

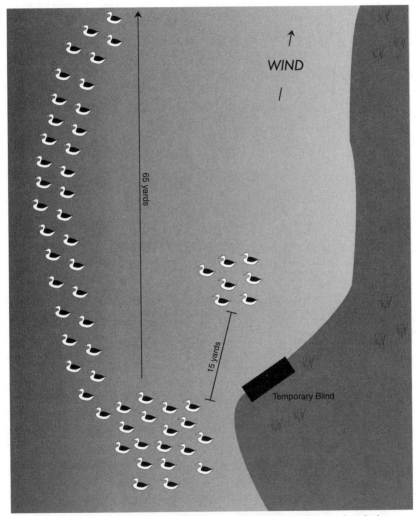

Shoreline sets for diving ducks. Look for a windswept shoreline with a little break of calmer water. Ducks will come along, see this setup, and land in the hole between the two decoy clumps.

ducks will be flying along a shoreline, and they'll come to a spot that offers some protection from the wind, however slight, and there are several ducks—or decoys—sitting there, and boom! They'll pop in on them before you have time to get your safety off!"

One other important point: Karnes prefers setting up where the wind is blowing parallel to the shore. His whole decoy strategy is built around a cross-wind. He moves around from one day to the next, picking his hunting sites to suit this criterion.

Karnes likes to shoot from the bank from a blind made out of reeds or brush, or he and his partners will simply sit motionless with their backs to rocks. "If there's some cover behind you, you have a face mask on, and you don't move when the ducks are coming, they won't see you, or they don't care. They'll barrel right in."

His diver spread consists of approximately 4 dozen magnum canvasback and bluebill decoys mixed together. First he sets a dozen decoys in a clump some 15 yards out from the downwind side of the blind. Then he moves to the upwind side of the blind and drops another, larger clump of decoys. (The open space between these two groupings is approximately 15 yards.) From this second group, Karnes runs a double line of decoys that curves outward and downwind, extending like a half-moon some 65 yards distant.

"If ducks are flying parallel to the bank and into the wind, and they come to that extended line of decoys, they'll almost always follow it in and land in the hole between the two clumps," Karnes attests. "Now if the ducks are coming downwind (from the other direction), when they see the line of decoys, they'll hook around it and sail right into the hole. So with this set, regardless of which way the ducks are coming, the shooting will be right in front of the blind."

Still, sometimes the birds don't land where he expects, and if this happens, Karnes is quick to adjust his spread. "The first couple of flights will tell you how the ducks are going to respond to the setup. If the first flight lands short, you can expect following flights to do the same thing, so don't wait to make your adjustment. Go on and do it right away. You might pull your decoys in closer to the blind or angle the curving line more—whatever you have to do to pull the ducks into good range."

Also, Karnes is quick to change hunting locations if he sees ducks working a nearby area better than the spot where he is set up. "That's one of the good things about not setting out too many decoys. You can pick 'em up and move quickly. And besides, you don't need all that many decoys for diving ducks. They're not the smartest birds in the world, and there's nothing complicated about pulling them in. If you just set out enough decoys to catch their attention when they're flying by, you'll have plenty of shooting."

Dave Zeug: Multi-rigging for Open-water Divers

As a game warden for the Wisconsin Department of Natural Resources, Dave Zeug's job is pursuing game-law violators. But in his off time, when duck season is in, Zeug prefers hunting for the bluebills, canvasbacks, mallards, and other ducks that raft up on 3,000-acre Shell Lake near the town of the same name. He follows these birds in a boat blind, moving around the lake to adjust for different winds and feeding conditions. He usually sets up along a reedy shoreline or adjacent to a point or an island where ducks are crossing.

Before dropping anchor, however, Zeug and his partner deploy their multi-rig, multi-species decoy spread, designed to toll ducks in over the big water. Zeug usually sets out 6 dozen decoys, predominantly bluebills, but also a few mallards, canvasbacks, redheads, buffleheads and/or goldeneyes, depending on which species are concentrated on the lake.

Zeug explains, "We've learned that we do a better job of pulling odd ducks if we've got a few of their species grouped together off to the side of the main spread so passing ducks can see and identify them." Thus his spread is comprised mostly of bluebill decoys in the center, with smaller groupings of puddle ducks and less common divers along the edges.

To set out this many decoys efficiently, Zeug uses a combination of multi-decoy lines and decoys that are strung and anchored individually. "We basically set a fishhook pattern in front of our blind. The long side of the hook is on the far side of the spread, and the short side is closer to the blind. The bend of the hook is upwind, and the two sides run downwind. With this design, ducks flying upwind hit the long outer string of decoys, then turn and follow it into the bend of the hook, which we arrange some 20 yards directly in front of the blind."

To set this spread, Zeug uses two multi-decoy lines, one twice as long as the other. Zeug's longer "mother line" measures 200 feet and is rigged to hold 20 decoys. The shorter line accommodates 10 decoys. These lines are tied from ¼-inch coarse, waxed nylon cord, and each has a 4-pound flat metal weight on one end only.

"We tie our lines so the decoys are fairly close (6 to 8 feet apart) on the end with the weight, and the distance intervals increase to 12 to 18 feet apart toward the other end," Zeug says. Decoys are attached via 10-inch drop lines with metal snaps and rings. The drop

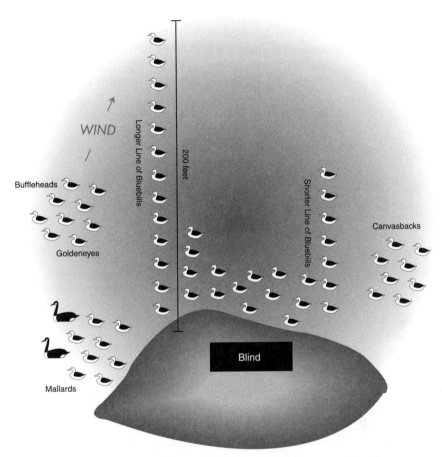

Multi-rigs for open-water divers. Fishhook pattern is created with two multi-decoy lines, one with 20 bluebill decoys, another with 10. The bend of the hook comprises 18 individually rigged decoys. Other decoy species are clustered outside of the main spread to attract odd puddle ducks and less common divers.

lines let the mother line sink below the water's surface, allowing a retriever to swim across it without becoming entangled. Having the line nearly a foot beneath the surface also keeps it from being visible to the ducks in the clear water where Zeug hunts.

Zeug keeps his mother lines wrapped around pegs on either side of the bow of his large johnboat, and decoys are stacked next to the line on the deck. To deploy a line, his partner drives the boat while he unwraps the mother line, snaps decoys onto the drop lines, and feeds the mother line and decoys overboard. The

©Bill Buckley

first step is dropping the mother line's anchor on the upwind side of their hunting site. Then they work downwind, snapping on decoys and peeling out line as they go.

The longer line is set out first, then the shorter line is set some 15 yards closer to where the blind will be. The upwind ends of the two lines are anchored side by side, then the long

Feeding the mother line and decoys overboard on a multi-decoy rig.

and short lines play downwind and parallel to each other. The downwind ends are left unanchored and free to swing in the breeze. Zeug completes the fishhook design by filling in between the upwind ends of the two mother lines with 18 individually strung and anchored decoys. Zeug tosses these out in a thick, curving band to form the bend of the hook. This upwind cluster of decoys will be the focal point of incoming divers, which usually sail in between the mother lines and land in the bend of the hook.

This arrangement forms the main part of Zeug's spread, but again, he sets smaller single-species groupings around this core. "I might put a dozen mallards on the left side of the fishhook and a family group of canvasbacks on the right side, then another small group of buffleheads or goldeneyes. I separate each group a few yards apart so there is a clear distinction between them. I also like to drop one or two Canada goose floaters out by the mallards as confidence decoys."

Zeug's single decoys are rigged with plastic (Tanglefree) line and wraparound lead-strip weights. He uses magnum decoys for maximum visibility, and he prefers weighted keels so that single decoys land upright when he throws them.

"With a spread of this type and size, we've got a chance to pull just about anything that flies by: divers, puddlers, big flights, little flights," Zeug says. "Our shooting is usually best in mid-October, when the nonbreeding adult bluebills are passing through. We call to them with a typical 'brrr, brrr' style, but calling doesn't really have that much effect on these birds. Instead, the decoys do the trick. They're visible enough for the ducks to see and be drawn to from a long way off, and the spread is arranged so they'll drop in right on our doorstep. When they do, things get really exciting!"

Russ Dyer: Rigging For Sea Ducks

Eiders and scoters offer sporty shooting along the New England coast, and Russ Dyer of Bowdoinham, Maine, has pursued these birds close to fifty years. A former chief game warden for The Pine Tree State, Dyer has done most of his sea duck hunting in Casco

Bay (offshore from Freeport) on one of the Calendar Islands.

"We usually set up on a 'half-tide ledge,' a rock outcropping on the point of an island that's exposed when the tide is halfway out. Our normal tides here run 8 to 12 feet, and when the tide is going out, many such half-tide ledges are exposed."

The sea ducks in this area—mostly common eiders and surf, whitewing and black scoters, with an occasional king eider or oldsquaw thrown in—feed around the islands on blue mussels in beds as deep as 70 feet.

"We move around a lot, picking our hunting spots according to the tide level, wind direction, and how rough the seas are," Dyer explains. The ideal spot is a pocket of water protected from the wind by a rocky point. "We'll set our decoys off the point, then shoot from the ledge with the wind at our backs," Dyer says. Usually he and his partners hide behind whatever natural cover is available. Sometimes they may pile up rocks or driftwood for a makeshift blind. Or occasionally they may hunt from a layout skiff anchored close to the point on its downwind side.

Dyer says sea-duck hunting coincides with the regular duck season, then extends several weeks beyond it. When the regular duck season is in, he sets out a combination of eider, goldeneye ("whistler"), and black duck decoys. During the sea ducks only season, he uses only eider decoys. Both eiders and scoters will toll to these decoys.

"Setting and picking up decoys in this area is difficult because of the rough, deep water," Dyer says, "so we don't put out a big spread. During the regular season, I'll set out a dozen eiders, a dozen goldeneyes, and 9 black ducks. That's a big spread. Then, when

we're hunting sea ducks only, I'll put out 12 to 14
eiders."

He emphasizes that these decoys are larger than
life for maximum visibility. "They're half again as big
as the real ducks are. Here we're hunting big open
areas, and we want decoys that can be seen from long
distance."

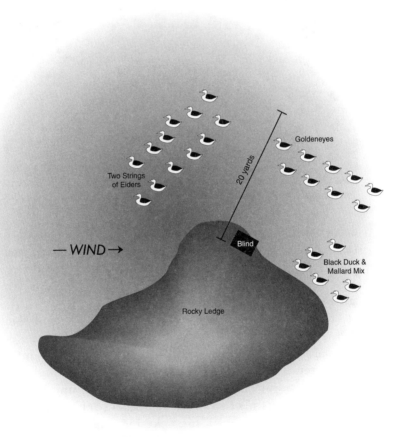

Sea duck rigs. In the regular duck season, multi-rigs of eider, goldeneyes,
and black ducks will help toll in a variety of species.

Dyer ties his eider and goldeneye decoys in multi-rig lines, 6 or 7 decoys to a line. He rigs with "pot warp" (heavy cord used to secure lobster traps) on the

Setting out multi-rig lines of eider decoys.

main line and window counter-balance weights (approximately 3 pounds) for anchors. "One thing you don't want is a weight that'll hang in the rocks. You need something with rounded edges and a smooth surface."

Dyer ties his decoys to this main line with 3-foot drop lines and snap swivels. This way, when the decoys are out, the main line is submerged 3 feet under the water. This allows a retriever to swim through the decoys without catching and dragging the line.

Dyer sets his decoy lines parallel to the shore and 20 to 25 yards out from his rocky hide. He staggers the lines to give the spread a random look.

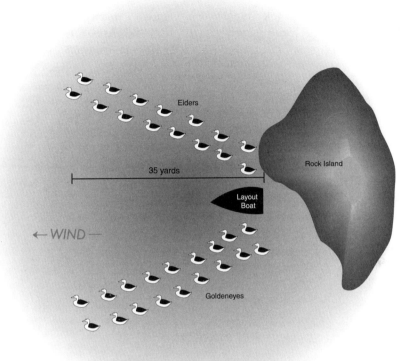

Eiders

Rock Island

35 yards

Layout
Boat

← WIND →

Goldeneyes

Sometimes Dyer hunts from a layout boat. When he does, he runs two arms of decoys—eiders on one side, goldeneyes on the other—with an open landing area in the middle.

When hunting sea ducks only, he uses two lines of eider decoys. "Sea ducks tend to come in low and land right in the spread. This is why most eider decoys get pretty shot up in the course of a season."

When the regular duck season is in, Dyer slightly overlaps his lines of eider and goldeneye decoys. Then

Decoys

he sets his black duck decoys closer in to shore. He rigs his black ducks with individual weights and strings.

One trick Dyer and his buddies employ is waving a white sheet to attract the attention of passing sea ducks. "Sometimes they'll fly way offshore in long lines of 200 to 300 birds," he explains. "When they see that white sheet waving, they may veer toward it, then see the decoys and come in, and that's when the fun starts!"

Chapter 4

Goose Spreads

In late September, when frosty mornings signal
the onset of winter in north-central Alberta, Canada
geese begin pouring through this region in unbeliev-
able numbers. These birds have nested in the Northwest Territories, and they're heading to wintering
grounds in Texas and New Mexico. For the next few
weeks, however, they will linger in this far-north farm-
ing area, gobbling peas, barley, and other grains scattered by the mechanical reapers that have collected most
of these fields' produce.

This is when the area offers some of the best
goose shooting in the world.

The area is remote, and hunting pressure is minimal. The geese are yet to be educated about the dan-
gers of double-clucks, black flags, and Big Feet. Instead, when they're coming to feed, they bore down on
decoys with the determination of long-haul truckers on
the homebound leg.

But don't make the mistake of thinking this hunting is a snap. Set up in the wrong place, put out a

shabby decoy spread, or don't conceal yourself properly, and you'll learn a lesson that's universal in goose
hunting. You can't be slack in this sport! Hunt hard,
hunt conscientiously, hunt smart, and the shooting can
be spectacular. But try to cut corners, and you can fail,
even in honker heaven.

In late September 1998, I spent three unforget-
table days hunting Canadas and mallards out of Canada
Maximas Lodge near High Level, Alberta. The sunrises at this thin latitude seemed to last forever. Each
morning's
sky was
awash in
shades of
gold, pink,
and peach,
usually bro-
ken by
wisps of
white cloud.
It was easy
to lose one-
self in this
beauty, to
revel in the
freshness of the subarctic and the prospect of what the
next few hours would bring.

Hunter brushes snow off Canada goose decoys
to keep them natural looking.

But daydream too long, and you'd be caught with
your pants down. This was because the mallards and
pintails would start coming soon after daybreak, huge
flights of birds swirling in from the river beyond the
trees along the edge of the field. If you weren't ready,
if the decoys weren't out and you weren't lying hidden
on the ground among them, you'd miss this first chance

of the day. And High Level, Alberta, is too far to travel to miss an opportunity.

The ducks would work our goose spread for about an hour. Then they'd go away. But we knew they were just the appetizer. Soon the main course would appear in the form of long, wavering lines of bigger birds. If the wind was right, we'd hear their honking sounds before we'd see them. The closer they flew, the quicker our hearts would beat, until finally, with wings arched and rocking and black feet extended below tannish gray bodies, they'd set into our decoys and we'd come up firing. When a hunter would connect, his target would thump the ground with a sound like a single, hollow beat on a muffled drum.

On this trip, outfitter John Leonard and his staff were masters at turning our hunting hopes into high-fives. They worked hard at locating birds and setting out lifelike decoy spreads. They spent the afternoons driving this region's backroads and pinpointing where geese were feeding. Then we'd be back there the next morning before daybreak. Everybody would help in getting the decoys out and arranging the layout blinds in a line, camouflaging them with stubble. Then the dawn would break, the daydreaming would start, the birds would come, and another page in our personal waterfowl journals would be written.

Goose hunting is truly a grand sport, in this or any setting. The majesty of these large waterfowl, the beauty and wildness of the places they inhabit, the excitement they inspire when they're locked on and coming—all of these things combine into a hunting experience unlike any other. From big Canadas in Oregon to cacklers in Texas to specklebellies in Louisiana to snows in North Dakota or Maryland, the thrill is electric when geese are on the glide slope.

Decoys

To lure these birds into range, hunters have devised a full menu of decoy spreads for different species and settings. On land and water, feeding areas and loafing sites, just the right decoy regimen is needed to overcome the usually wary nature of these birds. Here are brief looks at the spreads of seven of this continent's most successful goose hunters.

"Wicker Bill" Crist: Large Field Spreads for Canada Geese

Bruce "Wicker Bill" Crist has spent his adult life guiding hunters and fishermen, training dogs, training falcons, and running a taxidermy business in Ft. Pierre, South Dakota. It's an understatement to say that the outdoors is this colorful man's life. He's a bona fide expert in many fields, but if he excels in one, it's hunting Canada geese that winter on massive Lake Oahe and feed in surrounding fields of corn and winter wheat. "Wicker Bill" Crist's reputation for fooling honkers into gun range is legendary.

Crist hunts both from permanent pits and temporary decoy spreads that he sets up after locating where Canada geese are feeding. Mostly, he does the latter. "Scouting is the key to successful goose hunting," he says. "I drive backroads around Lake Oahe in the afternoon and watch for geese in the grainfields. When I find a concentration, I get a fix on their exact position, then I come back before dawn the next morning and set out my spread where the birds were feeding the afternoon prior."

Crist sets up either of two spreads, depending on whether or not new geese are in the area. "If there's been a recent migration and the geese aren't real wary, I'll set out 35 to 40 dozen decoys. But if I'm hunting birds that have been around awhile, and they're educated by the hunting pressure, then I'll set out up to 100 dozen decoys for more pulling power."

In both cases, Crist uses a fifty-fifty mix of silhouette and full-body decoys. When he's not hunting from a pit, he also uses 3 dozen magnum shells to conceal hunters lying prone in the field. The large shell decoys offer more cover than smaller shells.

Magnum full-body Canada goose decoys like these will add an extra element of realism to your spread.

Crist hauls his decoys in a custom-made trailer, which he drives right into the field. "Setting out 100 dozen decoys doesn't take as long as it sounds like it would," he assures. "Ten hunters can set out this many decoys in an hour."

"Wicker Bill" sets his goose decoys in an X pattern, with hunters lying in a line at the center of the X, facing downwind. This spread is thick in the middle and thins out in the arms of the X. He sets most of his full-body decoys downwind of the shooting line. This is

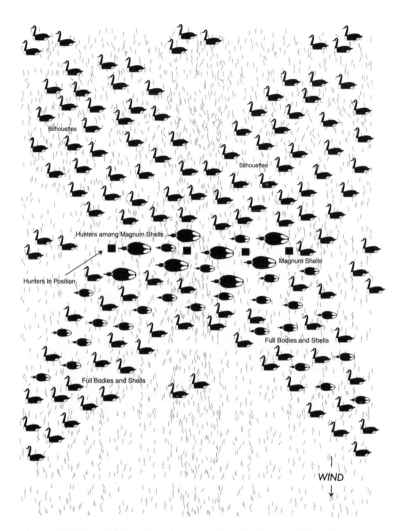

Large field spread for Canada geese. The shells and full-bodies are in the downwind side of the X pattern, because this is the direction from which most geese will come to land.

the direction from which geese will approach to land, and it's the part of the spread that should look the most realistic.

He positions most silhouettes on the upwind side of the spread, behind the hunters. "I make sure the silhouettes are set facing different directions, one quartering this way, one that way, one straight upwind, etc. Then, when geese are flying around the spread, they get an optical illusion of movement as some silhouettes appear and others disappear." He sets both full-bodies and silhouettes approximately 3 feet apart. "The main thing is to leave a good open landing area between the two arms of the spread on the downwind side," Crist stresses. "In a small spread (30 dozen decoys), this landing area might be 20 yards across. In a large spread, it'll expand to 30 to 40 yards."

When setting a large spread (100 dozen decoys) for "veteran" geese, Crist first sets out his main X pattern, then adds smaller groupings of decoys (2 to 4 dozen) at the top and sides of the main spread. He explains, "Geese that have been around awhile come off the lake in smaller bunches, so I include these

Lightweight and stackable, shells help make setting up a big goose spread a lot easier than it looks.

family decoy groups around the edge of my big spread for more realism."

Two other tips are to put a pair of full-body decoys square in the middle of the landing zone as a final lure for incoming birds, and to set an upright decoy 30 yards from the shooting line in each downwind arm of the X as a range marker. "I make sure my hunters know where these two decoys are, and that they shouldn't shoot until the geese are inside these markers," Crist stresses.

If snow geese are working the same area, Crist randomly mixes 3 to 5 dozen snow goose decoys into his large spread or 1 dozen into his small spread.

What if he sets his decoys out, then the wind shifts direction? "If we're close to the limit, we won't change the spread. But if we're just getting started, we'll move decoys to suit the new wind direction," says Crist.

One last trick this guide employs is "plenty flagging." He says, "I'll typically use 5 or more flags, but I don't want everyone flagging at the same time—just a little pop here, then another one there. This movement adds realism to the spread that passing geese find hard to resist."

Ron Latschaw: Small Field Spreads for Canada Geese

Ron Latschaw "let business get in the way" of his hunting. For twenty-six years, this resident of Grants Pass, Oregon, was a professional goose guide in the Columbia River basin of eastern Washington State. However, during the off-season, he began making and selling portable layout blinds that precluded hunters from having to dig pits each time they changed sites. Latschaw's business grew quickly, and today he builds and sells his Final Approach blinds and accessories full-

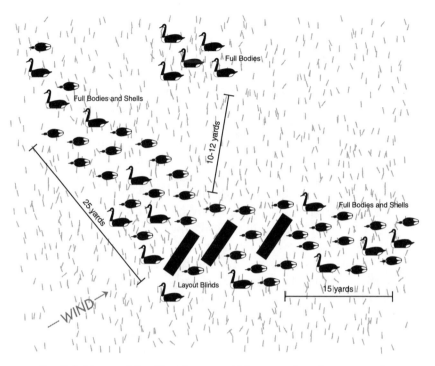

Small field spread for Canada geese. Using a modest decoy spread like this gives you the ability to change the setup if the wind shifts or the birds are spooky. An even smaller spread can work wonders later in the season when the geese are decoy shy.

time. Still, though no longer guiding, Latschaw continues to hunt Canadas several times each season.

He rarely sets out more than 75 decoys, and in the late season he may hunt over as few as 8. But numbers notwithstanding, he consistently decoys Canada geese into close gun range. He does so by setting up where the birds want to work, arranging his spread in a natural manner, then luring the geese in with judicious calling and flagging.

"I use the larger spread under normal hunting conditions, typically in the early to middle part of the season before the geese become decoy shy. But in the later season, after new birds have quit coming and we're hunting old veterans, I have better luck setting out only 8 or 9 decoys to simulate one small family group. This is sort of a 'finesse spread,' and it will pull geese that will flare off larger spreads."

First, the large spread. After picking his hunting spot, Latschaw sets out his layout blinds in a staggered row. He deploys up to five blinds, leaving 5-foot gaps between them. He places the blinds with the feet pointing at a quartering angle downwind. With this arrangement, geese flying upwind will approach at an angle to the blinds instead of head-on.

Next Latschaw sets out his decoys. On bright, high visibility days he uses mostly full-body and shell decoys. On overcast days he opts for more silhouettes. On "average" days he mixes full-bodies, shells, and silhouettes randomly. He positions all decoys facing into, quartering, or crossways to the wind—never facing downwind!

First Latschaw sets decoys around the blinds. "I'll put a couple of decoys between each blind, then I'll stagger other decoys behind and in front of the blinds, about 6 feet both ways. Next I'll extend a slightly curving arm of decoys out from each side of the main body of decoys (where the blinds are). The downwind arm runs out about 15 yards, while the upwind arm extends out about 25 yards. The overall design is a new-moon curve that bulges where the blinds are positioned."

Last, Latschaw places a half-dozen full-body decoys 10 to 12 yards straight in front of the blind that's farthest upwind. These decoys should simulate relaxed birds, with feeding or resting heads, not alert heads.

"With this setup, geese will usually swing down-wind, then turn, glide back upwind outside the arc, and set down around the family group," Latschaw explains. "The hunter in the upwind blind should call the shot. When the geese are right for him, they'll be square in front of the other hunters as well."

Latschaw uses a combination of calling and flagging to draw passing flocks' attention to his spread. "When geese are a long way off, one hunter calls and another stands and waves a flag as high as he can to get them to notice the spread. If the geese respond by coming, the flagger should get in his blind when they're about 300 yards out and cover up.

"The caller should continue to call. If the geese are acting like new birds, call 'em hard. But if they're reacting like old veterans, call sparingly. In this case, subtlety is better than pressure calling. You just have to use your judgment as to which style is best for each particular day and situation."

©Chuck Petrie

Hunters are camouflaged beneath camo tarps and super magnum shell decoys.

Latschaw adds that one great benefit in using a modest decoy spread and layout blinds is the ability to change the setup if the wind shifts, the birds are spooky, or only one or two hunters are getting all the shooting. "It only takes minutes to move the blinds and a few decoys to try a different setup," he says.

Late in the season, Canada geese frequently become decoy shy in areas where hunting pressure is heavy. Latschaw explains, "You'll have birds that lock up and look like they're coming, then they'll swing the spread at 80 to 100 yards and keep on going.

"This is when I go to a small decoy spread. I'll put only 8 or 9 decoys 15 yards straight downwind from my blinds. I'll hide the blinds thoroughly with natural vegetation. I won't overcall. I won't pressure the birds. I do everything I can to make 'em feel relaxed. Now you have to play their game instead of forcing them to play yours. A lot of times this finesse approach will work when using a bigger spread and loud calling will run the geese off."

Larry Smittle: Portable Open-water Set for Canadas

Larry Smittle of Eufaula, Oklahoma, believes quality is better than quantity when it comes to setting out a portable open-water decoy spread for Canada geese. Smittle, a retired sporting goods manufacturers' representative, achieves "quality" by using true-to-life decoys (G&H CF10 full-body floaters) and setting them exactly where working geese want to be. By doing so, he consistently enjoys up-close shooting over a mere 18 decoys.

"If you're where the geese want to be, this number is plenty," Smittle explains. "And if you're not where they want to be, picking up 18 is a lot easier and faster than moving a bigger spread."

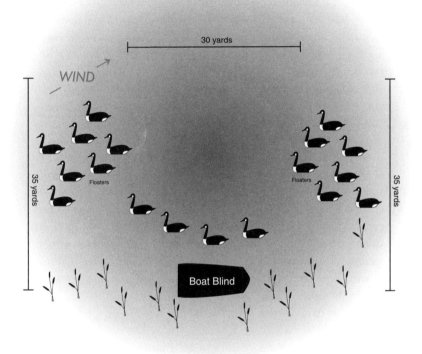

After feeding in nearby fields, Canadas will return to roost on lakes in small family groups, so a small spread like this will appear more natural than a larger one.

Smittle hunts on Eufaula Lake and Kerr Reservoir, two huge U.S. Army Corps of Engineers impoundments in east-central Oklahoma. Wheat and soybean farms surround these lakes, and the combination of food and open water attracts thousands of Canada geese each winter. The honkers rest and loaf on the lakes, and they fly out to feed in surrounding fields. Sometimes when they return, Smittle and his hunting partners are waiting.

"The shallow upper ends of both these lakes have some cattail islands, and the water depth on the flats around these islands averages 3 to 4 feet," Smittle says. "This is where the geese hang out between feeding periods."

Lack of hunting pressure in these areas is one of the keys to success. "The geese get pounded pretty hard out in the fields, but pressure on the water is light," says Smittle. "We make it a point not to hunt a given area repeatedly. We'll skip around between spots, or we'll wait for good conditions before we go hunting." Ideal conditions for hunting Canadas over water are a clear sky and a ten- to fifteen-mile-per-hour wind, preferably from the north, east, or south. "I do a lot of scouting, and I like to set up where a big group of geese is resting. We'll be on the water well before shooting time, and we'll have our decoys out when dawn breaks."

Smittle hunts from a boat, which he parks next to a patch of cattails with the sun at his back. His boat has a frame that he covers with Fast Grass, a commercial grass mat that causes his rig to melt into the natural vegetation. "We'll set up with the wind at our backs or crossing from left to right, but not coming straight on. But again, the number one concern is to have the sun at our backs. Being in shadows is crucial to keep the geese from seeing us."

Smittle says the honkers won't fly out to feed until full daylight. Then the birds will leave the water, stay out until mid-morning, and begin filtering back to the lake in small groups, typically four to six Canadas in a bunch. "This is why we don't use more decoys than we do," Smittle explains. "There may be a lot of geese in the area, but they sit around on the water in small family groups, so a smaller decoy spread is more natural than a bigger one."

First Smittle picks his hunting spot. Then he and his partners set their decoys by hand. "We can place 'em better by hand," he adds. "Might as well set 'em out right the first time," he explains with Will Rogers logic.

Smittle arranges his decoys in a modified horseshoe design. "We'll put a small grouping to the left of the boat, a second small grouping to the right of the boat, and we'll connect the two groups by a thin line of decoys closer to the boat."

More specifically, he sets 7 decoys in each grouping with approximately 30 yards of open water between the two clumps. The most distant decoy is 35 yards from the boat. Then he connects the groups by a line of decoys, 15 yards in front of the boat. "If we've got a wind that's crossing or coming from our back, geese will drop into the hole between the two decoy groupings," Smittle says. "Most of our shots come just as the birds are stretching their legs out to land."

Smittle rigs his goose decoys with heavy braided nylon line, and he anchors them with 8-ounce lead rings that fit around the decoys' heads for transporting. He says these anchors get a good grip in the soft lake bottom and keep the decoys from dragging when the wind is strong.

"One other thing: We're very cautious about our calling," Smittle adds. "When geese are heading our way, we don't call. Now if they start away, we'll get on 'em with our calls and try to pull 'em back. But as long as they're coming on, we keep silent. I know this is contrary to what a lot of hunters do, people who call loud and fast while geese are working. I won't tell you that they're wrong, but I will tell you that the silent approach works for us, and as long as it does, that's what we'll keep doing."

Billy Adams: Decoy Spreads for Fixed Open-water Blinds

Billy Adams of Richmond, Virginia, is ecstatic that Canada goose hunting in the Atlantic Flyway is coming back. Adams has guided and hunted honkers on the nearby James River and also on Delaware Bay in Delaware for twenty-five years, and when a moratorium on hunting these birds was imposed in 1995, he was devastated.

Now, though, Atlantic Flyway Canadas are rebounding from historic low numbers, and hunting is being phased back in. In 1999, a two-week season was allowed in the mid-Atlantic area, and six days of hunting was allowed in the Chesapeake region. Adams and others hope that more hunting will be forthcoming as the Atlantic population of Canada geese recovers.

A lot of goose hunting in these areas is done from fixed blinds on large, open tidal flats. That means hunters don't have the option of moving around to accommodate different wind directions. Instead, they must make the most of whatever wind is blowing by arranging their decoys to match that wind. Thus Billy Adams keeps his goose floaters in his boat, and each morning he sets them around his blind according to that day's wind direction. "I use 50 full-body floaters, and I'll set one of four rigs," Adams says. "The first is my 'no-wind spread.' The second is my 'crosswind spread.' The third is for when the wind is blowing from behind the blind. This is the best wind and the easiest to work geese on, since they're coming straight in our face. And the fourth is when the wind is blowing from straight in

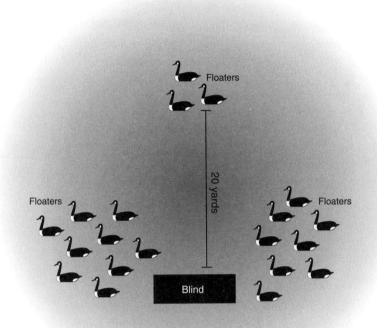

No-wind spread.

front of the blind. This is my least favorite wind direction, but I have a spread design to cope with it."

Adams sets his no-wind spread when calm conditions prevail or if he's not sure from which direction the wind will blow. "This is real simple. I'll drop 22 decoys in a group off the left side of the blind. Then I'll move around and drop 22 decoys off the right side. Next I'll drop the last 6 decoys right in front of the blind about 20 yards out. These are my

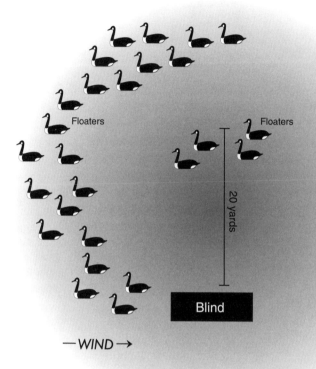

Crosswind spread.

leader decoys, and incoming geese will usually try to land between these and the bigger group on either the left or the right."

When the wind is blowing across the front of his blind, Adams drops the majority of his decoys off the upwind corner and curves them out and downwind in a C design. Then he trails a double line of decoys downwind approximately 20 yards in front of the blind. "This simulates a line of geese swimming into a bigger

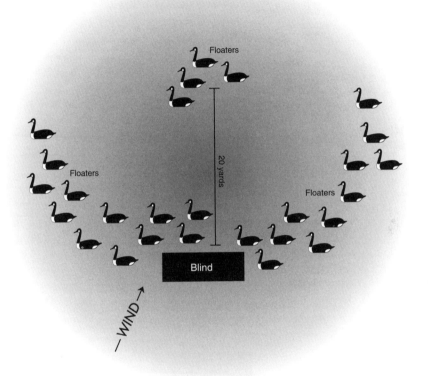

Spread for wind coming from behind the blind.

group. To work this spread, geese will sail upwind and land next to the main body of decoys and just beyond the line."

When the wind is blowing from the back of the blind, Adams drops his decoys in a C pattern with the outer arms extending downwind, and the middle of the C no farther than 10 yards from the front of the blind. Then he sets 5 leader decoys 20 yards in front of the blind by themselves. "With this setup, incoming geese

Decoys

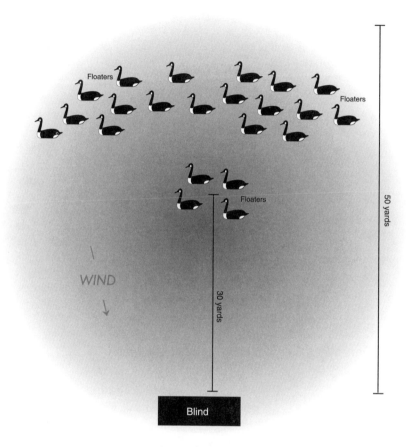

Spread for wind coming from in front of the blind.

will pitch around the leaders and land somewhere in the pocket (inside the C)," Adams explains.

And when the wind is blowing from the front of the blind, Adams groups the bulk of his decoys 50 yards upwind from the blind. Then he sets a half-dozen leader decoys 30 yards in front of the blind. Working geese come from behind the blind and usually land on either side of the leader decoys. "This gives you a going-away shot at their backs, but many times when the geese flare, they'll catch the wind and come right back over you, and then you've got a good overhead shot."

One special problem Adams and other tidal flats hunters face is rigging their decoys for strong currents and fluctuating water levels. "I rig with anchors that weigh 2 to 5 pounds apiece, and I have plenty extra line wrapped around the keels so that I can adjust the lengths for the water level I'm hunting."

Knowing how to toss out decoys so that they'll stay where you want them is also important. "I unwrap and adjust my line to the right length, then I'll throw the anchor out first with the decoy trailing," explains Adams. If you throw the decoy and anchor out together, the decoy may be out of position from where you want it by the time the anchor hits bottom and all the line plays out. You can be a lot more precise with placement by throwing the anchor first."

Don Stavinoha: Traditional Texas Rag Spread for Snow Geese

Don Stavinoha of Columbus, Texas, is a state trooper by occupation, but he's a snow goose guide by obsession. Stavinoha saves all his vacation, holidays, and compensatory time for the goose season, during which he guides for the Blue Goose Club in Altair, Texas. Stavinoha has guided for thirty years, averaging seventy days of hunting per season.

The Blue Goose Club — a commercial hunting operation some sixty miles west of Houston — is located on the Garwood Prairie, a major wintering area for snow geese, white-fronted geese, and lesser Canada geese. Each fall hundreds of thousands of these birds migrate here to feed on rice, soybeans, grass seeds, and other prime edibles. These birds roost at night on manmade holding ponds. Then they fly out at dawn to find grit and food. They usually feed until late morning, then return to their roosting ponds to loaf through the midday.

In mid-afternoon they fly back into feeding fields, stay until dusk, then return to their roost ponds. (Sometimes, if their feeding field has water in low spots or tractor ruts, the geese stay in the field all day, but they always return to their roost pond by night.) They may feed in a field next to their roost pond, or they may fly 20 or more miles away, depending on the availability of food.

Don Stavinoha and other guides scout extensively each afternoon during hunting season, looking for fields with big concentrations of feeding geese. He says, "I'll usually scout from 2:30 to 6:00 p.m. I'll average driving 100 to 150 miles to find where the geese are working. I like to find at least 5,000 birds in a field. If I can locate a rice field with this many geese using it, and most of them have their heads down feeding happily, then odds are high we can have a good shoot here the next morning."

Hunters dressed in white parkas will blend in with the rags and windsocks in this spread for snow geese.

When he's picked his site, Stavinoha returns well before dawn the next morning with his hunting party, and that's when the work starts. "We put out a white (decoy) spread with at least 1,000 pieces for a party of up to five hunters. If we've got seven or eight hunters, we might put out up to 1,600 pieces. When hunting snow geese, the bigger the spread, the better it is."

Even on close inspection, this snow goose seems fooled by the feeding decoy.

Stavinoah's "pieces" are squares of white plastic banquet cloth and homemade windsock decoys.

Stavinoha buys white banquet cloth in bulk rolls, and he cuts the plastic into square pieces approximately 30 by 30 inches. "I prefer the textured banquet cloth over slick plastic, since it doesn't have as much shine. Also, the 'rags' lose most of their shine after they've been used a few times and get dirty." Stavinoha carries these squares in a large sack. He can cram a thousand plastic rags in one jumbo bag.

The windsock decoys are made by cutting out large squares of banquet cloth, folding them into cone or bag shapes, taping the seams, then taping on pieces of thin cane for stakes. "In a 1,000-piece spread, I'll have approximately 700 plastic rags and 300 windsocks," Stavinoha says. "I'll transport these into the field with four-wheelers. It takes five men about an hour to put out a spread this size."

Decoys

The first thing Stavinoha does is outline the spread. "I'll take an armful of rags and start walking and dropping them on the ground to mark the spread's outer edges," Stavinoha continues. "I like to set a fish-hook pattern, with the shank (long arm) of the hook running upwind. The shank of the fishhook will be 40 to 60 yards wide, depending on how many hunters I have, and it'll run 150 to 250 yards long before bending back downwind."

In south Texas, prevailing winds are from south to east, so geese working upwind will be looking into the sun. "This is the perfect setup," Stavinoha explains. "Hunters sitting with their backs to the sun have their faces shadowed, so they're less likely to be seen by incoming birds."

While the guide outlines his fishhook pattern, the other hunters begin filling in the spread. "They follow along, scattering rags and fluffing them and sticking up the windsocks." By "fluffing" the rags, Stavinoha means shaking them out to full size, then draping or wrapping them around rice stubble to give them a three-dimensional effect. "Fluffed-out rags are a lot more realistic than flat or wadded up rags. Also, when rags are spread over the stubble, wind will cause them to move and create the illusion of live geese feeding on the ground."

The majority of the windsocks go in the downwind arm of the spread, explains Stavinoha. "I position my hunters within 10 to 15 feet of the downwind edge, so I use the windsocks as cover for the hunters. They can sit upright surrounded by windsocks, always wearing white parkas with hoods, and the height of the windsocks and the shadows they create will hide the hunters effectively."

The windsocks are always faced into the wind so that they will catch wind and fluff out. Besides hiding

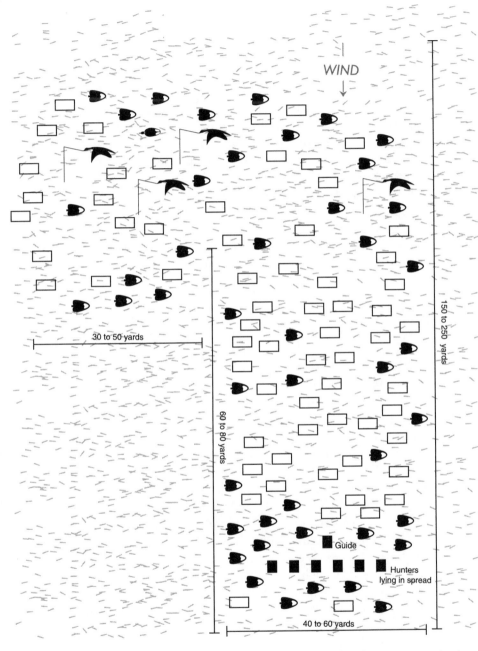

Traditional Texas rag spread for snow geese. Geese will aim for the open areas in the upwind part of the spread, giving hunters in the downwind edge close shots as the birds sail overhead directly into the wind.

the hunters, they also provide movement, which adds to the aberration of feeding geese on the ground.

Windsocks and rags are fairly dense (3 to 4 feet apart) in the spread's downwind arm, but Stavinoha prefers opening the spread up in the upwind part of the hook's shank, where it starts its bend. "This upwind portion of the spread should be ragged, with plenty of gaps and holes. Here I like to set rags to look like family groups with open spaces 20 to 30 feet between the groups. The idea is for incoming geese to spot these holes and aim for them. When they sail over the downwind edge of the spread, the hunters sitting there have overhead, close shots."

One other thing Stavinoha does if there is enough wind is fly 3 to 4 kite decoys in the upwind half of the spread. "I'll rig my kites on strings of different lengths, from 20 to 90 feet long. These provide movement and realism, and they also divert incoming geese's attention from what's on the ground. Snow geese are smart, and the more time they spend studying the decoy spread, the greater the likelihood they'll see something that'll cause them to flare away. So the kites help divide their attention when they're coming in, and this translates into better shooting."

Speaking of shooting, Stavinoha shifts his hunters around in the spread depending on where and how the geese are working. He explains, "To start out, they'll be lined up near the downwind edge of the spread. But if the geese are coming in on a corner or flying up into the gap of the fishhook, I'll move my hunters so that everybody can shoot. We can do this easily and quickly, just pull up a few windsocks, move to where the geese are working, form a new line, and stick the windsocks back up."

In Texas during the fall-winter season, the daily limit on snow geese is 20, and hunters may also bag two white-fronted geese and one Canada goose, so there is plenty shooting when conditions are good. "My favorite day is one with a ten-mile-per-hour wind, a dense fog, and a falling barometer," Stavinoha says. "This is what I call an ice cream day. This is when you'd better have some extra shells in your bag, because you're going to need them!"

Tommy Akin: Mixed Field Spread for Snows, Canadas, Ducks

Since 1991, Tommy Akin of Greenfield, Tennessee, and several friends have traveled to east-central Saskatchewan to jump-start their goose and duck seasons. Akin and his partners hunt snow and Canada geese and a variety of puddle ducks, all from the same dry field spread. After nine years of experimenting, they have come up with a decoy system that is amazingly effective and relatively easy to deploy.

"We go in late September or early October," Akin says. "The area where we hunt is the first stopover for snow geese migrating south from their Arctic nesting grounds. By the time they get to us, they've flown 1,800 miles nonstop, and they're ready for some groceries. They'll linger for several days, roosting on large open lakes in the area and flying out in the mornings and afternoons to feed in surrounding pea and barley fields. They feed in huge concentrations, tens of thousands in a field. In fact, we won't even hunt a field unless we feel there are at least 10,000 geese using it."

Akin and friends scout in the afternoon, driving backroads to trail geese from the lakes to feeding areas. "They're easy to follow," he says. "They fly out one wave after another. We just drive behind them until we see where they're going down. Once we have an exact fix on where they're feeding, we go find the landowner to ask permission to hunt the spot the next morning."

Akin says it's very common for Canada geese and ducks to be sharing the same field with the snow geese, and this has led to the evolution of their mixed decoy spread. "We've come up with a system that'll work on all of these birds," he explains. "Many mornings we'll take a combined bag of snows, Canadas, mallards, and pintails. In fact, this is the rule rather than the exception."

A magnum Canada goose decoy proves a fatal attraction for two Canada geese. Note the size difference.

The core of Akin's spread is 1,000 homemade white windsock decoys. "We designed our own pattern, and we had the windsocks cut out of white Tyvek (lightweight synthetic fabric) and sewn together by a local seamstress. Then we attached them to ⅜-inch wooden dowel rods for stakes. The socks have openings in the front that are 3 inches in diameter. When they catch wind, they billow out into the approximate size and shape of a live snow goose."

Roughly 1 in 25 of these decoys is sprayed with gray paint to look like a blue goose. Also, approximately 1 in 50 is fitted with a Herter's snow goose head atop the dowel stake for extra realism.

Akin says he alters the dimensions of the spread according to how many hunters he has. "If we have six hunters, we'll set our decoys out in a rough rectangle 60 yards wide (crosswind) by 40 yards deep (upwind edge to downwind edge). If we have more hunters than this, we'll make the spread wider and shallower so we can get all shooters in a line."

After deciding where to put the decoys, the next step is to mark the spread's outer boundaries. Akin explains, "We'll push a windsock in the ground at one side of the spread, then we'll walk off 60 or 80 yards —whatever we want—to the opposite crosswind edge."

Placing this next decoy is very important. It must be exactly crosswind from the first decoy on the other edge of the spread. "You want the wind blowing perpendicular to a straight line between these two decoys," says Akin. "This will ensure that geese will come in from downwind and work the whole spread. But if the spread is angled slightly off from straight downwind, the geese will come in on the corner, and then only one or two hunters will get all the shooting. So we take a lot of time testing the wind. We blow smoke or toss up dust. Exact wind direction can be tricky to determine in the predawn darkness, but we do our best to get it right."

Once these two decoys are set, other marker decoys are erected on the upwind and downwind edges of the spread. Then the space inside these markers is filled with decoys 3 to 4 feet apart. Also, all the windsocks must face into the wind so that they will catch the breeze.

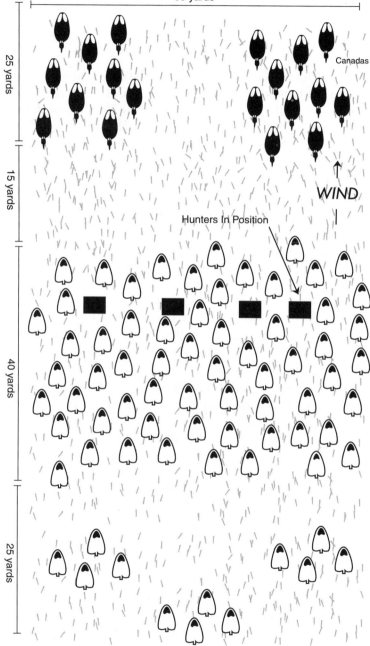

60 yards

25 yards

15 yards

40 yards

25 yards

Canadas

WIND

Hunters In Position

Mixed field spread for snows, Canadas, and ducks. Snow geese and ducks will come in and land among the white spread, while the Canada geese will land among the Canada decoys or in the space between the snows and Canadas.

"Once the main body is set out, we'll put 4 to 6 small family groups (3 to 8 decoys per group) on the upwind side of the main body," says Akin. "These groups will be separated about 15 yards from the main body and from each other. They simulate geese that have landed and are walking into the main body or birds that are feeding off by themselves. It's very common to see this situation with live birds."

Next Akin and partners set out their Canada decoys. "We use 4 dozen G&H super magnum shells and 3 dozen G&H Mirages on motion stakes. We set these starting at 15 yards from the downwind edge of

Hunter with a mixed bag of snow geese and mallards.

the snow goose spread and extending out to around 50 yards from the snow geese. We set these Canada decoys in two groups, one to the left and one to the right, leaving a 15-yard gap in between that funnels the birds to the middle of the spread."

Then Akin and his pals take up their shooting positions, on the ground in a straight line some 15 yards upwind from the downwind edge of the snow goose spread. "The snow geese and ducks will come in and land all around the white spread. The Canadas will usually land with the Canada decoys or in the gap between the snows and the Canadas. But if the Canadas start landing on the downwind edge of the Canada spread, we may move a couple of shooters down into the Canada decoys to take these birds, and the rest of us will stay back in the white spread."

Akin and his friends dress in white parkas and wear white facemasks. They sit on the ground on BackPack Recliners from Avery Outdoors, Inc. "We can sit upright among the wind socks and not be noticeable," Akin explains. "The BackPack seats give good back support, and you're up and ready to shoot when birds come in."

This spread takes around an hour for six hunters to set out and about half that time to pick back up. "We drive right to the hunting site, then carry the decoys out of the trailer in Rag Bag slings, also from Avery. One hunter can carry around a hundred windsocks, and he just walks along and sticks them in the ground and fluffs them out. It's really quick."

Obviously, this spread is more effective when the wind is blowing. "Wind is the key," Akin attests. "The best wind is fifteen to twenty miles an hour. If we can get a good breeze blowing and an overcast sky, maybe even a flake or two of snow falling, we'll wear 'em out. Considering the liberal limits on waterfowl in Canada, especially snow geese, a morning of shooting can leave you feeling like you've been in a boxing match."

Mervis Saltzman: Sparse Decoys for Specklebellies

Mervis Saltzman has spent more than six decades in waterfowler's paradise. Saltzman has lived his life in the heart of Cajun Louisiana, in the small town of Gueydan, where hunting ducks and geese comes as naturally as the Gulf breeze. Also, twenty years ago, Saltzman began making his Chien Caille ("Spotted Dog") duck and goose calls. Saltzman's white-fronted goose (specklebelly) call is widely considered one of the best in the business for luring these birds to the gun.

But good calling is ineffective by itself. Hunters must also hunt where these geese want to go, and they must set a natural-looking decoy spread to thwart the birds' suspicious nature. Through his years of pursuing them and studying their habits, Mervis Saltzman has become a master of all the skills needed to bag specklebellies on a consistent basis.

"We usually hunt 'specks' at the same time we're hunting ducks," Saltzman says. "I like to hunt in a rice field from a pit on a levee running north and south. I'll have water and duck decoys on the west side of the levee, and I'll have just a little water and specklebelly decoys on the east side of the levee. Specks like a field that's 'juicy,' with just enough water to pool up in the low spots between the clods."

Saltzman says that early in the season, before shooting pressure educates the geese, many hunters fare well on specks over a spread of 300 to 400 snow goose rags. However, it doesn't take long for the birds to learn to avoid the rags, and when he sees this happening, Saltzman changes his decoy tactics completely. He replaces the rag spread with a small number of specklebelly shell decoys set upwind from the pit and divided into separate family groups. "You've got to put your decoys out in a manner that will overcome the geese's caution," he explains. "I set my little family groups from 50 to 80 yards out in the field upwind from my pit. This looks real natural to specks, and they feel safer working in the wide open. But we arrange the spread so geese have to sail over our pit to get to the decoys, and when they do, we come up shooting."

Saltzman says prevailing winds in south Louisiana are from the southeast, east, and northeast. This is why he places the specklebelly decoys on the east side of the pit. "I might set one little family group (6 to 8 decoys) straight east of the pit at 50 yards, then another family group southeast of the pit at 65 yards, and a third family group northeast of the pit at 80 yards. This way, if the wind is blowing from any angle out of the east, there's a group of decoys that'll pull incoming geese straight over our pit. Also, the sounds of the call help to steer 'em over the pit."

Saltzman is very particular about how he sets his shell decoys. "I don't like the big full-bodies that stand up 6 to 8 inches above the ground. Live geese stay low and level to the ground when they're feeding. I set my shells on stakes about 3 inches above the mud. Any higher than this is too high.

"Also, I don't like more than one sentinel head decoy in each family group. I want the rest to be feeding heads, or maybe one 'semi' [upright resting position]. It's natural for all the specklebellies in a family group to be feeding except for one that keeps watch. If you've got half your decoys with upright sentinel heads, that's an alert. It's like something has scared them, and this may be enough to spook incoming geese."

One touch for extra realism may be the addition of 1 or 2 snow goose decoys staked out to the side of one of the specklebelly family groups. Saltzman explains, "You'll see this a lot, a single snow goose in the field with the specks. But they'll be out by themselves, never feeding in with the specks."

As the season wears on, Saltzman reduces the number of specklebelly decoys in his spread. "The spookier they become, the fewer decoys I'll set out," he says. "By the end of the season, I may only have 3 decoys out in one small family group, and I'll set them straight upwind from the pit about 75 yards away. I just do what I have to keep the geese from being suspicious."

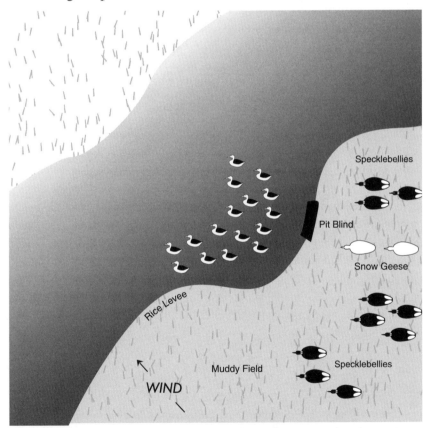

Sparse decoys for speckbellies. The specklebelly decoys are arranged in small family groups 50 to 80 yards upwind from the pit, giving the geese a false sense of security as they sail over the pit to get to the decoys.

Saltzman is a local legend for his ability to call specklebellies. "When they're a long way off, I start with two or three 'piercing calls' to get their attention. These aren't sounds that specks naturally make. They're just loud hail calls to make 'em listen and look. Then I'll start calling in regular specklebelly language, and I'll keep this up until they get close. I'll change to clucking, like the sounds the geese make

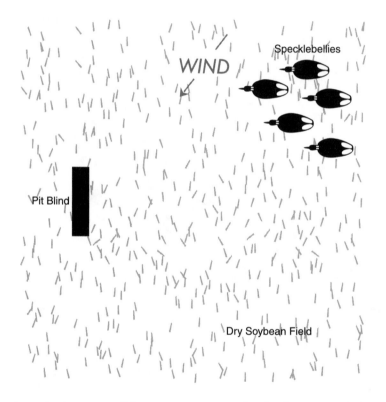

Later in the season, Saltzman uses even smaller family groups, which he places about 75 yards from the blind.

when they're feeding. Basically, I vary my calling in terms of volume and cadence, and I let the geese tell me what they like. When they respond to something, I just keep doing it until it's time to shoot."

The Higdon Finisher Canada goose decoy with moving head that mimics feeding goose.

Chapter 5

Movement

A few seasons back, my lease partner and two guests had been in our west Kentucky blind all morning without firing a shot. When I arrived at noon, they were grumbling about the warm temperature, overcast sky, lack of wind, and ducks that would make a couple of "courtesy circles" but wouldn't come in. "Local birds! We need to get some new ducks in here," my partner complained as he packed his shell bag to go home.

I'd come to our blind to set out a new dipper decoy in our permanent spread. It was the Higdon Finisher floating Canada goose, with a counterweight and pull cord to make it tip like a feeder. I'd recently seen a Finisher in another buddy's spread, and it added plenty of decoy and water movement when the wind was calm. I wanted to see how it would work in our hole.

After my partner and his friends had left, I rigged the goose in an opening in our spread directly in front of the blind. With decoys on the left and right, working ducks naturally settle into this void. I figured this was where the Finisher would be most noticeable to circling birds.

After stretching the pull cord back to the blind, I climbed in and loaded my shotgun. I had little hope of action. Most of our shooting in this cypress swamp comes in the morning, and conditions for this afternoon were about as poor as they could get. My main purpose for being here was to set the Finisher out for the next day's hunt. Still, I decided to hang around a couple of hours to see if anything would fly.

No more than fifteen minutes had passed when a lone mallard drake appeared outside the decoys, skirting the lifeless spread suspiciously. Instead of calling, I tugged on the Finisher's pull cord. The decoy's flexible neck stretched out as though the "goose" was feeding. Then with more pressure on the pull cord, the decoy tipped up—head underwater and tail in the air—and bobbed like a real Canada. This was all the convincing the greenhead needed. He cupped his wings, banked toward the Finisher, and sailed straight in. I'm sure he would have landed next to the decoy if I hadn't come up shooting.

In the next two hours I bagged two more mallards and a wood duck, all fooled by the tipping, bobbing goose. It wasn't a fast shoot, but it was far better than I'd expected.

This was the most graphic demonstration I'd ever had about the necessity of imparting movement to a decoy spread. Watch live ducks or geese on the water or ground, and they're usually in constant motion. Even resting birds stretch their wings, preen, swim, or walk around occasionally. Real waterfowl simply move a lot. This is why circling birds quickly become suspicious of a decoy spread with no movement. As they migrate down the flyway during fall and winter, they quickly gain an education in how to avoid "fake ducks."

Movement

Of course, adding movement to decoys is more important on calm days than on windy ones. When the breeze is up, decoys bob, swim, and waver like live birds. Also, incoming ducks and geese are less wary in gusty conditions. They may be buffeted around and may not get as good a look at the decoys. Who knows? For whatever reasons, a good blow is tantamount to an increased willingness to work.

On the other hand, calm air leads to greater scrutiny of a spread by circling waterfowl, and this is when decoy movement is critical. As in the example with the Finisher, when the wind is slack, imparting movement to decoys can mean the difference between having a good shoot and getting skunked.

Necessity is the mother of invention. In recent years, decoy makers and everyday hunters have devised a broad array of methods and products for adding "life" to a spread. Swimmers, tippers, shakers, flappers, jerk strings, kites, and flags are just a few examples.

And then there are the flashers. These decoys have battery-powered wings that spin around, rapidly flashing their dark and white sides, and they are the rage across the country. They do more than impart movement to a lifeless decoy spread. Ducks and geese can see this black-white flash from long distances and high altitudes. The motion is similar to that of a bird back-flapping its wings to land, and ducks especially are drawn to it like magnets.

These wing-spinners have been so effective that they have transformed marginal hunting spots into good ones and neophyte hunters into very successful ones. This, in turn, has raised serious questions. Are flashers too effective? Should they be restricted for the same reasons that electronic calls and baiting are banned? Such questions are being raised at this writing. These special decoys will certainly come under more scrutiny in terms of whether or not hunters will be allowed to use them in the future.

Regardless, the fact remains that a decoy spread with movement simulating that of real birds will lure ducks and geese into close range, while a lifeless decoy spread will attract few waterfowl. This is why savvy hunters will take advantage of whatever means are legal and available to include movers and shakers in their spreads.

Following is a review of do-it-yourself methods and commercial products for making decoys come alive.

Flasher Decoys
(Motorized Wing-spinners)

This new trend started in California's northern Sacramento Valley in 1998. For several years prior, hunters here had flown Turbo Kites over their decoys to attract passing ducks. The Turbo Kite is a child's toy, a Styrofoam disc kite that spins in the wind. Some innovative hunter discovered that by painting the slats on this kite black on one side and white on the other, they could imitate the alternating black-white flapping motion of a duck landing or taking off. Airborne ducks could see this flash from a long distance and were strongly attracted to it.

Flasher decoys were made to duplicate the spinning-flashing motion of the Turbo Kite. After several upgrades, the RoboDuk and Fatal de DUCKtion hit the market in 1998. Both of these used commercial decoys mounted above the water on poles and featured flat, outstretched wings spinning at about 250 rpms. Their power sources were built-in rechargeable six-volt batteries.

©David J. Sams/texasinprint.com

Fatal de DUCKtion flasher decoy.

These flasher decoys were an immediate sensa-
tion in California, and word of their effectiveness soon
spread throughout the country. During the 1999-2000
hunting season, manufacturers couldn't meet the huge
demand for their products, and hunters began making
their own flasher decoys from whatever parts they could
assemble. Hunters who had the first flasher in their
area usually had great success with it. However, as
the season wore on and more flasher decoys began
appearing (sometimes with multiple flashers in the
same spread), ducks began to grow leery of these
wing-spinners.

Will they continue to be as effective in seasons to
come as they were when they initially appeared? That
depends on where they are used, says Finlay Williams
of Marysville, California, who is the originator of
the RoboDuk. Williams says his experience is that
ducks may become wary of them where hunting competition is heavy and flasher decoys are commonly used.

However, he believes these motorized decoys will continue to attract ducks in other areas where pressure is
lighter and encounters with flashers are less frequent.

What are the chances of flasher decoys being
outlawed or restricted in some way? As of this writing,
several management agencies are collecting data to
determine if their use is detrimental to waterfowl populations and what, if any, restrictions might be appropriate. However, a moratorium on their use does not
appear likely in the near future. A spokesman for the
U.S. Fish & Wildlife Service says concerns over flasher
decoys "aren't even on our radar scope." It remains to
be seen whether their radar scope will light up.

In the meantime, a bevy of new manufacturers
will undoubtedly enter the flasher decoy market, and
their products will encompass many refinements over
original models, including remote control, which will
allow hunters to turn them on and off without leaving
the blind.

Robert Matthews: How to Use Flasher Decoys

Flasher decoys are easy to use, but hunters should
keep a few simple rules in mind when doing so, says
Robert Matthews of R&J Enterprises (maker of the
Fatal de DUCKtion decoy) in Marysville, California.

"Place your decoy where you want the ducks to
land, usually 15 to 20 yards downwind from the blind,"
Matthews instructs. "One common mistake hunters
make is setting their flasher decoy(s) too far away for
a good shot. Instead, keep it in close, and face it into
the wind just like a real duck would land." (To keep a
flasher decoy facing into the wind, tilt the stake back-
ward so that the decoy's butt is slightly closer to the
water than its front, and point the head upwind.)

Matthews says a flasher decoy should be erected 2 to 3 feet above the water. "Setting it up higher doesn't really offer any advantage," he says. "I've seen hunters set flashers on tall poles, but they don't gain anything by doing this."

Matthews believes that two or three flasher decoys offer more attraction to passing ducks than one. In this case, he recommends grouping the flashers close together instead of spreading them out. Also, he advises using poles of varying lengths to stagger the height of these decoys for a more realistic appearance.

Jerk Strings

Jerk strings are a simple, widely used method of imparting movement to a decoy spread. Basically, a jerk string is a line that runs from the blind or shooting site to one or more decoys in the spread that are anchored or tied firmly in place. When waterfowl are in sight, a hunter tugs on the line to make the decoys splash and bob around, thus adding motion and ripples on the water.

Jerk strings can be as simple as a line with one decoy attached or as intricate as a dozen or more on the same line. Some hunters rig jerk strings with a three-way swivel to run "splitter" lines to either side of an open shooting hole. Also, a commercial "Yank 'Em In" jerk string is available for purchase. This unit has a spring-loaded line holder, fits in a pocket, and is quick to set up. It is a good option for freelance hunters who move from one hunting spot to another.

Following are three variations of homemade jerk strings for both portable and permanent spreads.

Bruce Caldwell: Rigging a Tip-up Decoy

Real puddle ducks tip up to feed—heads down in the water and tails pointed skyward. A decoy rigged to emulate this same motion imparts both movement and the notion that food is available.

Bruce Caldwell of Mountain Home, Arkansas, routinely rigs one or more tip-up decoys when hunting in his home state or in neighboring Missouri. Caldwell's tip-up jerk string is simple, portable, and quick to deploy. He uses this rig in water that's wadeable, usually 1½ to 4 feet deep. (At least 1½ feet of water depth is needed so that the decoy can tip up.)

"My jerk rig includes 30 yards of stout tarred nylon string, two anchors, and a standard floating decoy," Caldwell explains. His two anchors are large concrete-filled soft-drink cups with a metal eyelet screw set in the top of each anchor. These anchors weigh 3 to 4 pounds apiece.

"I run the string from the blind to where I want my tip-up decoy positioned, where ducks can see it easily. I pass the line through the screw eye of the first anchor, then through the hole in the decoy's keel where the anchor string would normally be tied. Then I tie the end of the line to the screw eye in the second anchor. When the jerk string is arranged properly, the two anchors are a couple of feet apart on the bottom of the marsh, with the decoy floating above and between them."

With the jerk string rigged in this manner, Caldwell can tug on the cord and pull the decoy's head into the water. Then he can bob it and splash it like a real duck feeding, releasing the line so that the decoy will pop back to the surface in a normal floating posture. This bobbing, feeding action is a strong attractant to ducks eyeballing the decoy spread.

Rigging the tip-up decoy.

Caldwell continues, "One other thing I do is paint the butt of my tip-up decoy pure white so it'll flash in the sunlight. Ducks can see those white butts from a long way. When the wind is still, two or three tip-up rigs (one per hunter) are a real help in luring spooky ducks into close range."

George Cochran: Rigging the "Convincer" Jerk String

Pro bass fisherman George Cochran of Hot Springs, Arkansas, employs an intriguing jerk string variation. His forte is hunting greenheads in flooded timber. When he finds a hole the ducks are working, Cochran deploys his decoys (as explained in chapter 3), then rigs his "convincer" jerk string.

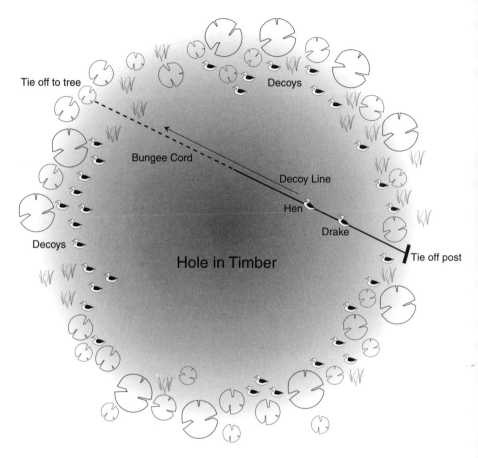

Decoys

Tie off to tree

Decoys

Bungee Cord

Decoy Line

Hen

Drake

Decoys

Hole in Timber

Tie off post

The "convincer" jerk string imitates a drake chasing a hen across the hole and is a magnet to circling ducks.

First he ties a 10-foot bungee cord to a tree trunk or concrete blocks (deposited before the season starts) on the upwind side of the hole. On the other end of the bungee cord he ties enough stout cord to reach completely across the hole when the bungee cord is stretched tightly. Next Cochran affixes two decoys onto this line. The first is a mallard hen, tied near the midway point of the string. The second, a mallard drake, is tied 3 feet back from the hen on the side opposite the bungee cord. Then Cochran "cocks" his jerk string by stretching it across the hole (like a big rubber band under tension) and tying it off to a convenient sapling or limb next to his calling and shooting spot. Then he waits for the opportune time to release it.

Cochran explains, "When ducks are circling the hole and looking down at the decoys, I untie the cord from the sapling and let it go, and the constricting bungee cord skis the hen and drake quickly across the hole. Then they hit the end of the cord and bob around on the surface. I think this looks like the drake is trying to catch the hen to mate with her. This really tears circling ducks up! Many times, when they see this, they lock up and fall right in. It's really effective."

Steve Fugate: Multi-decoy Jerk String for a Permanent Spread

For years, Steve Fugate of Paducah, Kentucky, has hunted ducks and geese on Mayfield Creek, a heavily used migration corridor near the junction of the Ohio and Mississippi rivers. Fugate hunts from a large floating blind on a flooded field adjacent to the creek. His decoy spread consists of some 500 ducks and Canada geese, which he leaves out through the season.

He says, "When the wind is light, a good jerk string can mean the difference between getting ducks and geese in and having them circle a time or two and go on. I rig several decoys on the same string for extra movement. All those decoys dancing around produce a lot of ripples. Waterfowl can see the contrast between calm water and the disturbed water around the decoys, and the movement looks like it's being made by live birds."

Fugate sets his decoys in two groups with an open landing area between them, directly in front of his blind. He runs his jerk string along one side of the landing area since the ripples will be more visible in the opening, and also because this is where circling birds' attention will likely be focused.

He starts constructing his jerk string by driving a stout post into the mud 35 yards from his blind, at the outer edge of his decoy spread. He drives the post deep enough so that the top is barely beneath the water's surface.

Next Fugate ties a 4-foot-long bungee cord near the top of the post. "You can get bungee cords cut whatever length you want at most tent and awning stores," Fugate says. "Such stores usually have the best bungee cords; they never lose their elasticity."

On the opposite end of the bungee cord, he ties a long length of Tanglefree (slick plastic) decoy line. ("I like this line better than nylon because it sinks down in the water when it's not under tension," Fugate explains.) He runs this line directly back to within a few feet of the blind. Then he attaches a length of green parachute cord, enough to run into the blind with several feet of slack left. He routes this parachute cord into the blind through a piece of ½-inch PVC pipe that extends through the blind's front wall and is attached to the floor of the blind.

Fugate screws a porcelain electric fence insulator onto the floor just behind and directly in line with the PVC pipe opening. The parachute cord is routed through the PVC pipe, then through this insulator, which allows him to pull the cord vertically with no friction or wear on the cord. The end of the parachute cord is then tied into a staple driven waist-high into the wooden frame of the blind. This secures the cord so

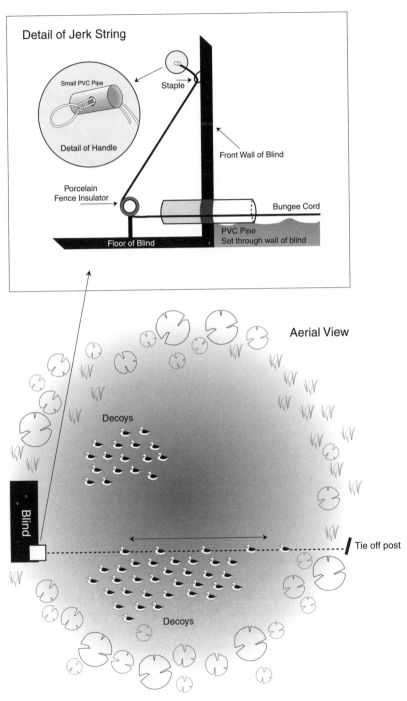

Detail of Jerk String

Small PVC Pipe

Staple

Detail of Handle

Porcelain
Fence Insulator

Front Wall of Blind

Floor of Blind

PVC Pipe
Set through wall of blind

Bungee Cord

Aerial View

Decoys

Blind

Tie off post

Decoys

This permanent multi-decoy jerk string is used to create ripples and stir up the water to attract distant ducks and should be pulled when the birds aren't looking directly at the spread.

that it can't accidentally be pulled out of the blind by a retriever or wading hunter.

Next Fugate affixes a pull handle onto the parachute cord (similar to a pull handle on a lawn mower starter rope). He uses a 4-inch length of ⅜-inch PVC pipe with a small hole drilled through the mid-point of the pipe (from one side to the other). Then he affixes this handle to the parachute cord at whatever point he wishes by doubling the cord, pushing it through the hole drilled through the pipe handle, then looping the cord around the pipe handle to cinch it down.

"If there's a good wind blowing, I won't need the jerk string, so I'll take the handle off and let all the slack out so the line will sink. This makes it easier for a retriever to get over it. Also, I let the slack out each day when I leave the blind. I've had trouble with beavers swimming into the line at night and chewing it in two. But if the line has slack, the beavers will swim over it without cutting it. Plus, if there's a heavy rain and the water level rises, the line won't break if it's got slack in it."

When it's time to hunt, Fugate pulls all of the slack out of his jerk string to make it springy, then he attaches his handle at knee height so that he can got an easy vertical pull of a couple of feet. The final step in Fugate's jerk string assembly is tying decoys onto the line. He usually ties on 10 decoys. "I space them evenly and cinch them onto the line with short overhand loops," he says. "I want the decoys snugged tightly to the line." Once tied, the decoys stay on the line through the hunting season.

Rigged in this manner, Fugate's jerk string is ready for use. When he pulls the handle, the bungee cord stretches and the decoys on the line "swim" toward the blind. When tension on the cord is released, the bungee cord retracts and pulls the line and decoys back toward the stake.

"I use the jerk string more to make ripples and stir up the water than to make the decoys actually appear to be swimming," Fugate says. "In fact, I don't jerk it when ducks or geese are looking at the decoys. When I see a flight coming, I'll start pulling with fast, hard jerks to make as many ripples as I can, then I'll quit when the birds get close.

"When they circle away from the decoys, I'll pull the string some more, then let off again when they turn back. I'll pull it whenever they're not looking and let it rest when they're inspecting the spread."

Flagging

Waving or shaking a flag is a proven trick for attracting the attention of distant geese. Sometimes such movement induces passing birds to veer toward the flagger, causing them to see a decoy spread they might otherwise have bypassed.

Then when geese draw near a spread, flagging can be used to simulate birds landing or flapping their wings on the ground. So at long range, flagging will capture waterfowl's awareness. When the birds are in close, it will impart movement to a lifeless spread.

Basic flagging can be done by attaching a black rectangle of cloth (3 by 4 feet) to a long, limber pole and waving it in broad sweeps when geese are passing at a distance. Flagging is usually accompanied by loud calling to get the birds' attention. Several hunters might use flags intermittently for more effect.

However, since this style of flagging is unnatural looking, hunters usually cease doing it when geese get close enough for a good look. Then they either lay their

©Gary Koehler

flags down and depend on calling and standard decoys to pull the birds in, or they switch to "landing flags" and continue using them until it's time to shoot.

Randy "Flagman" Bartz: Art and Science of Flagging Geese

Randy Bartz of Oronoco, Minnesota, is known as the "Flagman" because of his pioneering work in using flags to lure in Canada geese. Bartz has experimented extensively with flagging methods and flag designs. Today his Flagman brand products are used by serious goose hunters throughout North America.

"Back in the early 1980s, I was guiding for a goose outfitter in Rochester (Minnesota). We were using square black flags then, and they were good at long range, but they'd scare geese that got in close," Bartz says. "So I set out to develop a flag that would duplicate the wing action of landing geese, something that would be an aid instead of a detriment with close-working birds. I didn't start out intending to commercialize my products. I was simply trying to come up with something that would improve my own hunting."

Bartz designed his T-Flag, with outstretched wings supported by a dowel rod through the flag's center and another limber rod stretching from wingtip to wingtip. When held by the end of the main rod and whipped up and down with wrist action, the flag's wings flap realistically like a landing goose. He learned that when geese were scrutinizing his decoys, he could flap his T-Flag from high overhead down to the ground, simulating a goose alighting in the decoys, and this would convince the live birds to follow suit.

Eventually Bartz refined his T-Flag, making two other models. His Lander flag has more of a live-goose profile and a white crescent across the back, offering extra realism for close-working Canada geese. His Pole Kite flag is made for use with a fiberglass fishing pole to wave at geese at long distances.

After two decades of experimentation, here is how Bartz uses his flags for gaining the attention of geese and drawing them in close. "When the birds are a long way off, I'll hold my Pole Kite high overhead and whip it back and forth to flap the wings aggressively. It's the same wrist action as jigging a fishing rod. I make a lot of motion to try to get the geese to notice it.

"If they turn my way, I'll continue using the Pole Kite until they spot the decoys and start descending toward them. Then I'll stop flagging and refrain from doing so as long as the geese keep coming. But the second they start sliding off or showing any reluctance to come, I'll pick up the Lander and give 'em a quick look, just three or four flaps, and I'll put it down. Then I just keep showing them the Lander as much as I have to to keep 'em coming."

Bartz continues, "In a sense, flagging is like calling. Some days you have to call more, some days less. Some days you have to flag more, some days less. You have to experiment with different approaches to see what works best. Now remember that I'm calling at the same time I'm flagging. But I'd say the flag is more important than the call. It makes a spread come alive. It creates an illusion of real life."

Bartz adds that while flagging is mostly used on geese, it also works on ducks. "The principle's the same. Ducks are attracted by the movement, and this leads them to the decoys. So flagging is a way to change ducks' minds about where they're going and to pull them in your direction instead."

Bartz frequently includes a few goose decoys in his duck spread, so using a goose flag isn't out of place. But he's also experimenting with prototype duck flags, and his results are promising. "I'm mostly showing these on a long pole, and they're very effective at pulling ducks from longer distances," he says.

Kite Decoys

Flying kite decoys over a spread is another way to draw waterfowl's attention and convince them to come. Kite decoys are made from very lightweight material—typically Tyvek. They are designed to fly and tip like a real bird in the slightest breeze. Kite decoys are available in Canada and snow geese and mallard ducks. They are mostly used in field spreads to hunt geese, though they are becoming increasingly popular in shallow-water spreads for duck hunting.

Kites are used two ways. The first is the standard kite method, using a crossbar kite (like a child's kite) and a long string. A wind in the seven- to fifteen-miles-per-hour range is ideal. The height this kite flies depends on string length. Also, it flies with a static, hovering look.

The crossbar kite has two drawbacks. One, the wind must be blowing before it will fly. (If a kite is flying and the wind slacks, the kite will come down.) And two, in a strong wind the crossbar kite makes a slapping, rustling sound that may scare close-flying waterfowl.

The other kite decoy is the type that is flown from a fiberglass or bamboo fishing pole (15 to 20 feet long) erected vertically in the spread. A length of metal rod is driven into the ground with approximately a foot of the rod left exposed above ground. Then the hollow pole with the kite decoy (attached with monofilament fishing line) is slipped down over the metal rod, which holds the pole upright. When the breeze blows, the kite flies behind the pole like a real bird hovering over the spread. These kites usually have a more natural look and wing-flapping motion than crossbar kites.

Jim Cripe: Tips for Using a Kite Decoy

Jim Cripe of Spokane, Washington, is president of Outlaw Companies, maker of Outlaw decoys. Cripe has broad experience developing and using kite decoys to hunt waterfowl. "From long distance, kites create more movement than you can imagine," he says. "They're extremely effective at gaining birds' attention and steering them to your decoys."

He offers the following tips on how and where to employ pole kite decoys. "I generally rig my kites with about half as much monofilament line as the pole is long. In other words, when a kite is hanging straight down, I want the tail even with the midpoint of the pole. You don't want the kite hanging down far enough to touch the ground or the water."

Cripe erects his kite(s) at or close to the upwind edge of his decoy spread. "Working birds will home in on a kite, then they'll peel off and circle to find a landing spot. So by setting my kites upwind and positioning my hunters a few yards downwind from them (in the front or middle of the spread), they'll have good shots as the birds sail overhead."

Cripe says several kites in a spread multiplies the beneficial effects. "In a big field setup, the more movement your spread has, the more attraction it has. In this situation, I'll typically scatter three or four kites along the upwind edge of the spread."

One trick that can be deadly is erecting a kite pole next to a hunter in a pit or layout blind. Then when incoming birds get close, have the hunter take the pole in hand, lift it off the metal rod, and lay it down slowly, thus "landing" the kite among the decoys. Live birds will frequently follow the kite to the ground. "It's easier to do this with a shorter pole, say a 12-footer," Cripe advises.

Does a kite hanging vertically beside a pole in a calm wind spook live birds? "Nobody's ever told me a kite hanging down has scared birds away," Cripe answers. "Of course, it's not doing any good in this situation, but any slight breeze will cause it to fly. We typically put our kites up before we start hunting and leave them up until we go home."

Flier Decoys

Flier decoys serve a similar purpose as kite decoys, except these attach directly atop tall stakes instead of trailing behind them on strings. Flier decoys provide the illusion of live geese or ducks about to land in the spread. Some are constructed from lightweight cloth (Goose and Duck Magnets, Goose Noose) and flutter noticeably in a slight breeze. Others are molded from heavier plastic (Carry-Lite Flying Mallard and Canada Goose) and have mounting springs for ¾-inch dowel stakes so that they will rock side to side in a breeze.

©Bill Buckley

Flier decoys are more effective when several are set together, simulating a flight of landing birds. Stakes should be different lengths (4 to 8 feet) for realism's sake. Flier decoys should be set facing into the wind and upwind from where hunters anticipate shooting at incoming geese or ducks.

Windsocks

Windsock decoys are used primarily in field spreads for hunting geese or ducks. When a breeze is blowing, these lightweight socks puff out with air and work back and forth like live birds scurrying about looking for grain or grass. They are frequently used with silhouettes to provide movement and a third dimension among those flat, non-moving decoys.

Windsocks must always be set with their openings facing the wind. If the wind shifts, these decoys must be adjusted so that the wind can keep them inflated.

©Wade Bourne

Wing Flappers

Another unique way to add movement to a goose spread is by attaching wing flappers to the backs of full-body or shell decoys. These attachments include frames and lightweight fabric wings that flutter in the slightest breeze (Rogers Decoy Wings, Flapperz).

Another varia-tion of the wing flap-per is the decoy with mechanical wings that are activated by tugging on a pull cord. Examples in-clude G&H's FBWE goose decoys, Higdon Motion De-coys' Finisher Flap-per Silhouette decoy, and Flyway Ani-mated Products' Deceptor goose and duck decoys.

©Ron Spormer

Commercial Motion Decoys

Commercial manufacturers make a broad range of decoys and related products to impart movement to decoy spreads. These include swimmers, dippers, wobblers, splashers, and other gadgets run by batter-ies, pull cords, and wind power. All of these products have the same purpose: to create decoy and water move-ment on days when the breeze is down and the spread is unnaturally still.

Following are brief descriptions of several motion decoys and products currently available. In each case the name of the manufacturer is included, and more information can be obtained through waterfowl supply catalogs.

Avery Wave Maker. Available in floating duck and feeder models, Wave Makers feature a stainless steel pendulum with an offset head that offers superior movement and lifelike water ripples. The motor operates for thirty hours on one alkaline C battery.

Cabela's Goose Walker Swivel Base. This spring-loaded swivel base attaches with a Velcro strap to any full-body self-standing goose decoy. When the wind is blowing, it allows the decoy to move with a side-to-side action. It is most natural when used with a decoy with a feeder head.

Decoy Heart. This round plastic housing encloses a small battery-powered motor that is designed for insertion into a hollow plastic decoy. (Cut a flap in the back, insert the Decoy Heart, turn it on, close the flap.) A rotating weight in the motor causes the decoy to wobble and produce ripples in the water.

Expedite Moto Magnet I, Moto Magnet II, Moto Magnet II Ultra. All Moto Magnet units are motorized stakes designed to make a goose decoy move back and forth vertically, like a live bird reaching over for a bite, then raising back up. The Moto Magnet I is designed for full-body decoys; the Moto Magnet II for shell and silhouette decoys. The Moto Magnet II Ultra is a Moto Magnet II with a remote control. All systems require two AA batteries for operation.

Expedite Quiver Magnet. The Quiver Magnet is a motion system designed for floater duck decoys. It is a round plastic housing enclosing a small battery-operated motor. The Quiver Magnet is designed to be placed inside a hollow plastic decoy. (Cut a flap in the back, insert the Quiver Magnet, turn it on, close the flap.) A rotating weight in the motor causes the decoy to wobble and produce ripples on the water.

Expedite Quiver Magnet H$_2$O. This floating water shaker looks like an oversized hockey puck. It has an internal water-resistant motor (AA battery-powered) and an attachment for an anchor cord. Three or four of these scattered through a small decoy spread will produce ripples like real ducks make when feeding and resting.

G&H Mirage Motion Decoy. This stackable shell decoy has amazing detail, and its Motion Stake includes a spring device that allows this decoy to wobble with a side-to-side feeding motion in the slightest wind.

Herter's Ultimate Torpedo Decoy. Herter's Ultimate Decoy is fitted with a motorized "turbo" keel attachment that produces a swimming and wave-making action. The removable motor is powered by one AA battery. Also, Herter's sells a Twin-Turbo decoy with double the power of the  Torpedo. Plus it offers Torpedo Motor Kits and universal mounts to fit other brand decoys.

Higdon Finisher Floater Goose Decoy. This floating goose decoy (Canada or snow) comes with a pull cord, a flexible neck, and a unique counterweight-swivel system to allow it splash water and tip up like a live feeding goose.

G&H Mirage Motion Decoy.

Higdon Finisher Motion Field Decoys. These full-body and shell goose decoys have pull cords, flexible necks, and stakes. When a hunter in a nearby pit or blind pulls the cord, the decoy will appear to feed or preen with lifelike realism. Also, up to six Finisher Motion decoys can be operated simultaneously by a battery-powered cam, or up to four decoys can be operated simultaneously by a hand-operated cam.

Motovator. A product of the Feather Flex division of Outland Sports, the Motovator is a soft foam mallard decoy mounted on a rigid foam base that houses a small electric motor (powered by two nine-volt batteries). As the motor's armature spins, this decoy wobbles and produces ripples.

Pulsator. From Paducah Shooters Supply, the Pulsator is a Flambeau Mallard Feeder (Duck Butt) decoy mounted atop an electric bilge pump. A power cord runs from the anchored Pulsator to a control box in the blind, then to a twelve-volt battery. When the switch is turned on, alternating pulses of current cause the bilge pump to spurt water from beneath the decoy, making it bob and splash like a real feeding duck. Two Pulsators may be run via a splitter off the same power cord. Four Pulsators may be operated off one control box and battery.

The Mallard Machine. Maximum splash and water movement are provided by this three-arm molded frame that supports three decoys and a submerged trolling motor in the middle. The Mallard Machine is battery-powered and comes with a 100-foot power cord and switch. When the trolling motor is turned on, the thrust is toward the surface, thus churning the water and creating ripples and movement in other decoys in a wide radius.

The Real DeCoy. A&M Waterfowl, Inc., makes four models of The Real Decoy: Swimmer, which is propeller driven and swims in a circle; the Flutter Duck  and Flutter Goose, which are floating decoys that wobble side to side; and the Feeder, which is a vibrating duck butt decoy. All are battery-powered. All anchor as regular decoys, except the Swimmer requires a swivel to prevent line twist.

Wonderduck Paddle Wheel. This floating decoy offers a combination of dual paddle wheels to splash water and rotating wings to capture passing ducks' attention. In a nutshell, it's a motion machine. Two or three of these decoys, coupled with one pole-mounted Super Wonderduck flasher decoy, provide a strong attraction to ducks that are wary of large spreads of stationary decoys.

Parting Thoughts on Decoy Movement

One of the more enjoyable facets of waterfowling is conjuring up new ways to improve hunting success. Duck and goose hunters are innovators and tinkerers. Each season, most hunters try something new, attempting to improve their bag of birds over the previous year. Frequently these involve how to make decoy spreads more natural looking and convincing to live birds overhead.

In this regard, there is no known end to the variations of jerk strings, moving decoys, etc., that imaginative hunters have come up with. I know a guide on Reelfoot Lake in west Tennessee who has rigged a "flying decoy" that he can trigger by remote control that slides down a piece of heavy monofilament line from a nearby tree to land in his decoys. He says circling ducks frequently follow this imposter right in.

I've seen a jerk rope attached to a wooden pallet counterweighted so that it floated just under the surface. Talk about moving water! Pulling the pallet back and forth underwater created a small tidal wave in the decoys.

Then there was my own oddball method of creating decoy movement while reaping another highly prized benefit. When I maintained a big open-water spread on Lake Barkley in western Kentucky (see chapter 3: "Open Lake Doughnut Hole Spread"), the flat where my floating blind and decoys were located bordered a submerged creek channel on two sides. The outermost decoys in my spread were anchored at the very edge of the drop-off into the creek.

One day I decided to hang fishing lines off the back of the decoys' keels, bait them with minnows, and try to catch some crappie. I rigged a dozen decoys with lines that hung a couple of feet off bottom. Then each morning I'd bait the hooks with shiner minnows and head to the blind to wait for ducks to fly and crappie to bite.

It usually wasn't long before a decoy would start bobbing, then another and another. If the wind was slack, I'd leave the fish on the hooks to keep the decoys moving. Sometimes a big crappie would stay active for an hour or two. Then when the fish tired out and the ducks weren't flying, I'd go out in the boat and collect my catch and rebait the lines.

Looking back, it was a strange way to fish and a novel way to add movement to my decoys. And catching those crappie was almost as much fun as luring mallards in over the open water!

Chapter 6

Rigging

It was an exercise in frustration and a test of my religion!

I was hunting ducks and geese on a river near my home in Tennessee. I was on the river because a prolonged freeze had locked up all the shallow swamps and flooded fields in the area. The river offered the only option to birds that were feeding in dry cornfields in the morning, then seeking open water for loafing through the midday.

I knew I'd made a good decision when I launched my boat and started running to find a hunting spot. I flushed ducks every few hundred yards—mostly mallards, twenty here, fifty there. I estimated one flight at more than a hundred, and this was where I decided to set up. If so many birds liked this spot, others would too. I'd toss out my decoys exactly where the ducks had been sitting. Then I'd pull my boat in next to the bank, set up the portable blind, and get ready to shoot.

The plan was sound, but there were two flaws in how I carried it out.

Decoys

The anchor lines on my decoys weren't long enough, and my weights weren't heavy enough. The river was more than 20 feet deep where the ducks had been resting. I'd anticipated this, and my lines were long enough for the weights to touch bottom with a couple of feet to spare. But there was strong current in the river from a recent heavy rain, and the concrete Dixie cup weights were too light to hold the decoys with their lines stretched almost vertically.

So they started dragging downstream. And the ducks began working like crazy as my spread headed round the bend!

I quickly took down my boat blind, motored out, picked up the decoys, and brought them back up to my hunting spot. I threw them out closer to the bank, hoping the bottom might be shallower and they'd hold.

It wasn't, and they didn't. By the time I got the blind set back up, the decoys had begun traveling again. And of course, big flights of mallards were now swirling over the river, pitching to my vagabond decoys that had quickly drifted back out of range.

How could I solve this dilemma? I considered hopscotching my boat blind downstream to stay abreast of the decoys, but they were scattered too far apart for that to work. I thought about finding some large rocks along the shoreline and tying them to my decoy lines, but that would take too long.

Finally I decided to pick up the decoys again and cut the lines and anchors on some to add more length and weight to others. This worked, but by the time I finished re-rigging, the ducks had almost quit flying. I wound up bagging a couple of strays, but I had missed the main part of the flight.

There is a postscript to this story. I was back on the river the next morning, and this time my decoys were rigged with longer lines and heavier anchors. I went back to the same spot and tossed my decoys over-board, and this time they stayed put. When the ducks started showing up, a friend and I shot easy limits, plus two bonus Canada geese that glided into our goose floaters. This satisfying morning was a complete con-trast to the previous frustrating one.

Rigging decoys properly can make a big difference. Most hunters rig decoy lines and weights without much thought—tie 'em up and toss 'em out. However, there is a broad range of rigging options available that can make a spread more efficient and convenient to use.

A decoy rig (combination of line, anchor, and associated hardware) should meet two basic require-ments. First and most important, it should hold the decoy where the hunter places it. And second, a rig should be easy to work with—that is, as hassle-free as possible. The best decoy rigs are those that are simple to deploy and take up, and that minimize problems such as tangling and lost time.

Following are different ways to rig decoys for shallow or deep water, calm or rough water, permanent or portable spreads, and individual or multi-decoy lines. There are many options in terms of line, anchors, hard-ware, knots, etc. Hunters who know the right rigs for their particular hunting situations will be more effec-tive, and they will experience fewer problems in de-ploying decoys for ducks and geese.

Straight-line Rigging

"Straight-line rigging" is the term for the stan-dard one-decoy, one-line, one-anchor rig. This is the most basic rigging method in waterfowling, used by the vast majority of hunters who set out a floating spread.

Straight-line rigs can be used by walk-in hunters carrying decoys in a backpack, by river or lake hunters running in a boat to find ducks and geese, and by fixed-blind hunters who put out spreads of dozens of decoys. Thus straight-line rigging involves many variables in terms of type of line, length of line, style and size of anchor, and hardware. A straight-line rig for shallow, protected, soft-bottom marshes should obviously be different from that used for deep, wind-blown, hard-bottom lakes.

Here are explanations of the various components of the straight-line decoy rig and when and how to use them.

Decoy Line

Any line can be used to connect decoys to anchors as long as it is strong enough not to break and its

strength isn't affected by exposure to water. Still some lines are much better suited for rigging decoys than others. They are more durable, take knots better, are easier to deploy and retrieve, and are less likely to tangle. Following are descriptions of popular decoy lines and their advantages and disadvantages.

Rigging

Nylon line. This synthetic line is used by more waterfowl hunters to anchor decoys than any other material. Nylon line is strong, rot-proof, plus it sinks, holds knots well, is available in drab colors, and is relatively inexpensive.

Nylon line comes in two varieties: twisted and braided. Twisted nylon line usually has three strands that are simply twisted together. In comparison, braided nylon line has eight or twelve strands that are interwoven and stitched tightly together. Braided line is far more desirable as decoy line than twisted line. Braided line won't unravel, while twisted line will. Braided line is also much more abrasion-resistant and holds knots better than twisted line. Braided line's drawback is its cost: two to three times more than twisted line. Still, in the small quantities used by most waterfowl hunters, the benefits of braided nylon are worth the extra expense.

Nylon lines come in size numbers. The smallest size hunters should consider for anchor lines is #18 (.058 inch diameter, 165 lb. test). More commonly used sizes are #36 (.085 inch diameter, 320 lb. test), #42, #48, and #60 (.116 in. diameter, 560 lb. test). These larger sizes offer overkill in strength, and they're easier to handle in cold, wet conditions.

Braided and twisted nylon lines come in a number of hunter-friendly colors, including olive drab, tan, green, and black.

One suitable option to braided line is twisted nylon line that is covered with a tar coating. The tar decreases nylon line's slickness, making it "grab" knots better. It adds to the line's abrasion resistance, and it gives the line more stiffness, making it easier to handle. Its dark brown color blends in with marsh bottoms. Tarred, twisted nylon in sizes #36 to #60 is good line for decoy anchors, but the ends should be burned (nylon strands melted together) and knotted with a simple overhand knot to keep the strands from unraveling.

Tangle-resistant line. Extruded PVC lines are catching on with more waterfowl hunters. This rubbery green line (O-ring material) comes in several commercial brands: Tanglefree, Avery Knot-Proof, H.S. Quik-Rig Decoy Cord. Its main selling point is its resistance to tangling. Decoys with short anchor lines (4 feet or shorter) don't even have to be wrapped when packed in a decoy bag. The decoys can be bagged with lines and anchors hanging loose; then they can simply be dumped out of the bag without entangling other lines or decoys.

Tangle-resistant lines will tangle when lines are longer than 4 feet, but the tangles are much easier to pick out than tangles in other types of line. Pull, yank, and shake, and the tangles fall out. Tangle-resistant lines are convenient and strong. They won't rot. They are dull green in color. They sink rapidly. One drawback is their cost—approximately twice as much as braided nylon.

Tangle-resistant lines don't hold knots well, so line crimps or anchors with built-in crimps are a must. Crimps are small metal or plastic locking devices through which line is routed and doubled back, then mashed tight to keep the line from slipping. Crimps are used to secure tangle-resistant line to decoy keels, anchors, and hardware.

Two special anchor systems are available with these lines. The Tanglefree company sells its own torpedo-shaped lead anchor (4 ounce) with predrilled holes and a molded-in crimp for permanently securing the line to the anchor. (Excess line should be trimmed flush with the side of the anchor to avoid snagging other lines when decoys are bagged.) Anchor lines are cut to desired length. One end is secured to the decoy keel with a crimp, and the other end is attached to an anchor.

Another anchor system available through Avery Outdoors, Hunters Specialties, and Feather Flex (Outland Sports) is an adjustable rig that uses a push-button (spring-loaded) cord lock (like that used on parkas to cinch down rain hoods). Tangle-resistant line is cut longer than normal, and an anchor is attached with a crimp at one end. The other end of the line is passed loosely through the line-tie hole in the decoy keel. Then the push-button cord lock is run down the other end of the line. Rigged in this manner, line can be pulled through the keel hole to adjust for desired length, then the cord lock can be set to hold the line at that length. Also, when picking decoys up, you can pull the anchors up tight to the decoy keels and secure them with the cord locks. The decoys can then be bagged with excess line hanging loose and the lines won't tangle.

Overall, tangle-resistant line offers many benefits in terms of convenience and time saved in setting out and picking up decoys. It is especially recommended for freelance hunters who hunt different water depths from one day to the next.

Monofilament line. Monofilament (heavy fishing line) is used by some waterfowl hunters for anchor lines but is far less desirable than nylon or tangle-resistant line. Monofilament isn't as easy to work with, is slick, and is more vulnerable to abrasions than nylon. Its main virtues are its low visibility and its resistance to tangles (in high pound-test sizes). Monofilament line might be considered by hunters for use in ultraclear water, but in other cases, braided nylon or tangle-resistant line is better.

Parachute line. Thick nylon parachute line is a good option for hunters needing highly durable anchor lines. Many open-water hunters who leave their decoys out through the season use parachute cord in olive drab or brown. Parachute line is prone to tangle, but its large diameter allows tangles to be picked out with minimal effort. Parachute line holds knots well. Ends should be burned to prevent unraveling.

Other lines, wire. Cotton, jute, and other lines from natural fibers aren't recommended for anchor lines. These generally aren't as strong and don't last as long as the synthetics. They are okay for temporary use if better lines aren't available, but they can't be expected to hold up.

Some hunters occasionally use electrical wire, thin metal cable, or other materials for anchor lines, but these usually aren't available or practical for widespread use.

Anchor Types

Decoy anchors can be anything that sinks and is heavy enough to hold decoys in place: railroad spikes, bricks, large washers or hex nuts, old spark plugs, fishing sinkers, tire weights, etc. However, through the years innovative waterfowlers have devised a variety of molded lead anchors specifically for decoys, and these generally work better than the "make do" anchors listed above.

The variety springs from the different places and conditions in which decoys are used. Some designs and sizes are better in a shallow, soft-bottom marsh. Others are more suitable for open water, rivers, sand or rock bottoms, etc. Thus hunters should learn about different anchor designs, then rig with those that best match their particular hunting situations.

Following are descriptions of decoy anchor types and applications to which each is best suited. Sizes given are those listed in major waterfowl supply mail-order catalogs.

Strap anchor. The strap anchor is a long, thin, pliable lead bar designed to wrap around a decoy's neck to secure anchor and line while the decoy is transported. This anchor is best suited for shallow to medium-depth water where currents and wind aren't excessive. Since this anchor is not designed to dig into the bottom, it will slide in strong currents or wind, thus is it not recommended for use on open water. Instead, strap anchors are best suited for freelance hunters who set portable spreads in shallow marshes, flooded timber, etc. Strap anchors are available in 4-, 6-, and 8-ounce sizes.

Strap anchor.

Over-the-head anchor. This anchor is a flat lead disk (like an Oreo cookie) with a wire loop molded in for securing the anchor over a decoy's head. This is a multipurpose weight suitable for calm water and light to medium chop. Resting upright, this weight is resistant to skidding across bottom. If pulled sideways by wind or current, the edge of the weight digs into the bottom. Standard size for over-the-head anchors is 8 ounces. One drawback to this anchor is its tendency to chip decoy paint during transport.

Neck ring anchor. This is a round or oblong collar-type weight that loops over a decoy's head for transport. This anchor lies flat and provides a good grip, especially on a soft bottom. This is another good choice for portable spreads and decoys toted in bags, though neck ring anchors will slip off occasionally and cause tangles. One variation includes "ears" that extend out from the corners of an oblong ring, like an H with an oval in the middle instead of a crossbar. These ears are for adjusting line length for different depths. Line is wrapped around the anchor for storage, then

Neck ring anchor

unwrapped and cinched around one of the ears when the length of loose line matches the water depth. Another variation of the neck ring anchor has a flattened edge opposite the line tie hole that digs into the bottom if the anchor starts dragging. Neck ring anchors come in 8-, 12-, 13-, and 16-ounce sizes. They are a good choice for freelance hunting on open water.

Wrap-around anchor. Similar to the neck ring anchor with "ears," this design is an H with two crossbars instead of one. A large quantity of line may be wrapped around the bars, hence the name. Then line may be unwound to any desired depth and cinched around a corner of the anchor to keep more line from unwrapping. This makes the wrap-around anchor good for setting portable spreads, especially in deep open water (rivers, lakes). This anchor lies flat on bottom and has good resistance to dragging. Its main drawback is that smaller wrap-around anchors cannot loop over a decoy's head to secure line during transport, and bigger ones that can loop over the head are hard on paint jobs. This anchor is available in 8- and 16-ounce sizes.

Mushroom anchor. The name is in the shape. This classic boat anchor design comes in small models for decoys. Sizes range from 4 ounces to 2 pounds. (This heavy mushroom is used for anchoring the end of a multi-rig line in heavy chop.) When pulled sideways, a mushroom anchor tilts and digs into bottom. Mushroom anchors are more frequently used in open water, though the smaller sizes are fine for shallow, confined waters. This anchor's main drawback is its lack of a way to be secured to the decoy during transport. If it unwinds from around the neck or keel, a tangle will result.

Mushroom anchor

Two-in-one anchor. This is a strap anchor with a small mushroom on the end opposite where the line is tied. Thus this anchor can be wrapped around a decoy's neck for transport, eliminating the possibility of tangles. Then when the anchor is straightened and deployed, the mushroom digs into bottom if the decoy starts dragging from wind or current. This is a versatile anchor system for freelancers who hunt in a variety of settings. It comes in 6- and 8-ounce sizes.

Pyramid anchor

Pyramid anchor. Again, the name describes the shape. This compact pyramid of lead digs into the bottom when pulled sideways. It is available in a 6-ounce size, which is fine for protected waters but is too light for choppy water or strong currents. Also, this anchor lacks a built-in method for securing to the decoy during transport.

Grapple anchor. This special anchor is similar to a mushroom anchor, except it has tapered claws that will grip virtually any bottom: gravel, rocks, sand, silt, mud, etc. This anchor comes in 8- and 16-ounce sizes. Its best use is in deep open water, where maximum holding power is needed. A special folding grappling anchor (24 ounces) is a good choice for anchoring a multi-rig line in open water.

Decoy Hardware

Decoy hardware includes an assortment of snaps, clips, and swivels used for three primary purposes: (1) the quick connection and disconnection of decoys to a straight-line or a multi-decoy rig, (2) elimination of line twist, and (3) the quick placement and removal of line sections to adjust anchor line length.

Some hunters rig anchor lines with the anchor at one end and a large snap swivel at the other end. They keep the decoys and lines separate, then snap the lines into the decoys' keel holes to set them out and unsnap them when the hunt is over. They do this both for convenience and to allow the decoy to turn without twisting the line.

Grapple anchors

Other hunters rig in reverse: one end of the line is fastened to the decoys' keels, the other to a snap swivel. Then anchors are snapped on as the decoys are deployed. When the dekes are taken up, anchors are detached and put in one pile and decoys and lines are placed in another pile.

The main use for hardware is in rigging multi-decoy lines, which is discussed later in this chapter.

One note on hardware: Don't buy small, inexpensive snaps and swivels used for fishing.

Snap swivel

Purchase large (easier to work with), high-quality brass or stainless steel hardware available through waterfowl supply catalogs. Bigger hardware is easier to operate with cold hands, and it's also more durable.

Knots

When using nylon line, good knots are a must to secure line to decoys and anchors. (Again, crimps should be used with tangle-resistant line.)

One of the best knots for this purpose is the slipknot. This knot is simple and fast to tie, and it won't come undone. Start by passing the line through the decoy's keel hole or anchor tie. Next tie a simple overhand knot in the end of the line to serve as a stop when the slipknot is cinched down. Then tie another overhand knot around the line on the other side of the keel or anchor. Slide this knot against the keel or anchor and snug it tightly against the knot in the line's end.

Another good knot for nylon line is the fisherman's improved clinch knot. This knot takes more effort than

©Dit Rutland, DU

Improved clinch knot and slipknot.

179

the slipknot, but it is stronger and more secure. Pass the line through the keel hole or anchor tie. Wrap the tag (short) end around the long end five times, then pass the tag end back through the opening between the bottom-most twist and the keel or anchor. Last, pass the tag end between the main line (twists) and the loop running from the top to the bottom of the twists. Pull the line tightly from both directions to set the knot.

Decoy Straight-line Rig Considerations

Anchor size. Anchor size is governed by common sense. The more force pulling against a decoy, the heavier the anchor must be to keep the decoy from moving. For instance, a duck decoy in heavy wind and waves requires a heavier anchor than the same decoy in a quiet marsh (assuming line length and anchor shape are the same).

For a hunter wading into a marsh or beaver pond, 4-ounce anchors are adequate. For general use, 6-ounce and 8-ounce anchors are the consensus choice. For big open water or rivers and tidal flats where current is strong, 12-ounce, 16-ounce, or even heavier anchors may be needed to keep decoys from dragging.

Anchor coatings. Some anchors are made with a soft plastic material completely coating all lead and metal surfaces. The purpose of this coating is to cushion anchor-decoy contact and to prevent anchors from scratching or chipping a decoy's paint during transport.

Anchor line length. The more slack line a decoy has, the more likely the anchor is to hold. This is because more slack line allows the decoy to pull against the anchor at a greater angle, and the anchor gets a better grip to hold against wave action or current. So how much slack is enough? That depends on location, water depth, wind, waves, etc. Decoys in shallow, protected waters need less line slack than decoys set in deeper, wind-exposed areas since dragging forces aren't as great.

A good rule of thumb for freelance hunters who change spots frequently is to rig decoys with 6 feet of line for shallow marshes, flooded fields, flooded timber, etc. This will be suitable for water from a few inches to over 5 feet deep, which will cover most freelance situations. (Using 6-foot lines in 6 inches of water is awkward, but it's better than having 4-foot lines and wanting to hunt in 5-foot water.)

Freelancers who hunt open rivers and lakes should rig with much more line and anchor weight, depending on depth, current, and wind exposure in areas they will be hunting. They should wrap extra line around anchors or decoy keels, then adjust the amount of line each time they set up. (This can be done by half-hitching line around anchors or hooks in the front of decoy keels or by simply looping line around decoys' necks to keep excess line from unwinding.) Four to 6 feet of slack is a good rule of thumb in these situations. However, hunters who set out decoys with this much slack and leave them overnight should expect tangles the next morning.

Anchor lines in permanent decoy spreads should have less slack so that they won't tangle. Hunters who put out permanent spreads around fixed blinds will know precisely how deep the water is. Thus they should take this depth, add a couple of feet of line so that the decoys can swing freely (and to accommodate for rises in water level), and tie their anchor strings to this length.

Decoys

Then by setting decoys more than 2 feet apart, they will avoid tangling with other anchor lines when the wind shifts and the decoys swing about. (Hunters deploying a permanent spread can use heavier anchors since they won't be setting out or picking up each day.)

Making Your Own Decoy Anchors

Do-it-yourself waterfowl hunters can mold their own decoy anchors, saving money while enjoying the satisfaction of using products they've made. Following are instructions for molding concrete and lead anchors.

Concrete Anchors. Pouring small concrete decoy anchors is easy and economical. Hunters can pour several dozen concrete anchors in a couple of hours, then have them ready for use two days later.

Necessary ingredients include: one bag (80 pounds) of concrete mix, one 50-foot roll of sixteen-gauge galvanized clothesline wire, paper cups, water, a five-gallon plastic bucket, a trowel or small spade, heavy-duty wire pliers, and brown concrete tint (optional).

First, cut 8-inch sections of galvanized wire. Bend the wire in the middle to form a loop, then twist the two ends together two or three turns. Make one wire loop for each anchor desired.

Next, line paper cups up on a flat surface and put one wire loop beside each cup.

Pour approximately 5 pounds of dry concrete mix into the bucket, then add water a little at a time, stirring concrete and water together with the trowel. Continue adding water until concrete mix is the consistency of pancake batter. Also, if brown anchors are desired for camouflage purposes, add tint to this mixture of concrete and water, and stir thoroughly. One tablespoon of tint will be plenty to color this much concrete.

Use a large rigid cup or scoop to pour the wet concrete into paper cups. When a cup is filled, insert a wire loop into the concrete twisted ends first. Jiggle the wire loop to work the twisted ends close to the bottom of the cup and to stand the loop up straight. Continue filling paper cups until all concrete mix is used up. Then repeat the process if more anchors are desired. Don't try to mix too much concrete at once, since it might start setting up before it can be poured into the paper cups.

Leave the concrete-filled cups overnight to harden, then peel the paper cups away from the anchors the following day. Allow the anchors to air cure an additional day for maximum hardening. Concrete sets up better in hot weather than in cold, so this is a job better suited for summer or early fall than for winter.

One option to the above "recipe" is cutting the wire pieces longer (approximately 15 inches) so that the loop will hang around a decoy's head. This will keep lines from unwrapping and tangling while the decoys are being transported. However, concrete anchors rubbing against decoys are tough on paint jobs. For a freelance spread that will be set out and taken up frequently, lead over-the-head anchors or strap anchors are a better alternative.

Concrete anchors may be made in different-sized paper cups. Small anchors are sufficient for quiet waters and no current. Big anchors are necessary for open water where wind or current are more likely to drag decoys.

Lead anchors. Do-it-yourselfers can mold their own lead anchors with minimal investments in time, effort, and expense. Anchor molding equipment is offered for sale by several outdoor mail-order companies. Melting pots, ladles, and anchor molds are available in a number of styles and sizes.

Molten lead is very dangerous, and great care should be exercised when pouring anchors. Wear gloves with leather palms to protect against burns. Wear a sweatband to keep from dripping sweat into molten lead. Work outside or in a well-ventilated shed. Wear a dust mask to avoid breathing fumes. After working with lead, wash your hands thoroughly before eating or drinking.

Lead can be found in tire stores (old tire balancing weights), scrap yards, plumbing supply houses, and other building supply sources. When melting old tire weights, skim steel rim clips and any impurities from the top of the molten lead.

Homemade anchors can be fashioned by pouring molten lead into muffin tins. Use large fence staples for line ties. Prior to pouring lead, turn the staples point-up and tap the points with a hammer to bend them down. Then, using needlenose pliers, hold the staples points-down in the middle of the muffin spaces and pour molten lead around them. Or arrange lengths of wire over muffin spaces, and hang staples over the wire so that the points extend far enough down to be enveloped in the lead when it is poured. When the lead hardens, the turned-down points will prevent the staples from pulling out.

For duck decoy anchors, fill small muffin tins halfway. For goose decoy anchors, fill tins to the top.

Multiple-decoy Rigs

A multiple-decoy rig (also known as a "trotline rig" or "gang rig") is a long line anchored on one or both ends with several decoys attached. The purpose of the multi-decoy rig is to allow hunters to set out and pick up a sizeable spread more efficiently. Especially in deep water, it's faster to set one line with several decoys on it than to set an equivalent number of decoys rigged straight-line style. Also, multi-decoy lines are anchored with weights from 1 to 5 pounds, so they stay put in strong winds or current.

This rig is traditional for hunting diving ducks on deep or rough open waters of the upper Midwest and Northeast. (See Dave Zeug and Russ Dyer sections in chapter 3.) A multi-decoy rig is also ideal for setting a spread on a deep river. (I now use multi-decoy lines on the river described in this chapter's introduction.) Some hunters run multi-decoy lines in shallow water, but straight-line anchor rigs are usually better in this situation.

A multi-decoy rig consists of a main line (called "mother line"), an anchor line and anchor on each end of the mother line, and drop lines spaced along the mother line for attaching decoys. These drop lines are usually 12 to 15 inches long, so that the mother line is suspended this far beneath the surface. This keeps it from being visible to incoming waterfowl, and it prevents retrievers from becoming entangled as they fetch downed birds.

Multi-decoy rigs can be purchased ready-made (just add anchors and decoys), or hunters can tie their own rigs. Commercial multi-rigs typically handle 6, 12, or 18 decoys set approximately 8 feet apart.

How to Tie a Multiple-decoy Rig

By tying their own multi-decoy rigs, hunters can customize mother line length, anchor line length, number of decoys, space between decoys, etc., to suit their desires. Following are instructions for tying a 12-decoy multi-rig line with decoys at 8-foot intervals and anchor leads measuring 15 feet long.

Materials needed include: 120 feet of large diameter (⅛- to ¼-inch) tarred nylon line for the mother line (this line should be heavy duty and stiff for ease of handling and resistance to tangling), 18 feet of standard-weight braided nylon decoy cord, twelve small snaps (like a dog collar snap; purchase at hardware store), twelve small metal rings (size of a quarter; purchase at hardware store), twenty-four large plastic cable ties (purchase at hardware or auto parts store), two anchors, (2 pounds or more each), and 12 decoys.

Start by stretching the mother line out in the yard. Then tie an anchor on one end of the mother line.

Measure back up the line (from the anchor) 15 feet, and attach a cable tie. Cinch it down tightly so that it won't slide along the line.

Next go to the far end of the line, pass the end through the ring in a snap, and slide the snap down the line flush against the cable tie. Then affix another cable tie 1½ inches up the mother line from the first cable tie. If done correctly, the snap will be trapped between the two cable ties but able to slide freely between them. (Check to make sure that the snap's ring is not large enough to slip over the cable ties.)

Now measure 8 feet up the mother line and attach another set of cable ties and snap in this manner, continuing until all twelve snaps are secured onto the mother line at 8-foot intervals. Then tie the second anchor on the other end of the mother line. Next tie a

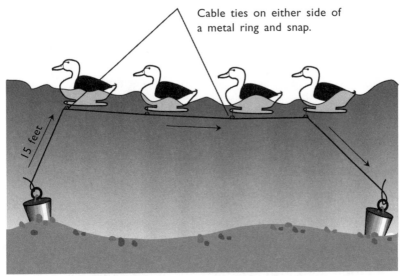

Cable ties on either side of a metal ring and snap.

15 feet

Multi-decoy rig. Decoys should be spaced at 8-foot intervals.

15-inch length of decoy line directly to each decoy's keel. On the opposite end of this line, tie a metal ring.

Now the multi-decoy line is ready for deployment. Start by determining where you want your closest upwind decoy positioned. Idle the boat slightly upwind or upcurrent from this point, drop out the anchor, and begin feeding out the mother line as the boat drifts or idles downwind or downcurrent. As each snap on the mother line comes up, attach a decoy by snapping in a ring on the end of the decoy line. Then toss the decoy overboard. Continue this process until all 12 decoys are out. Then stretch slack out of the mother line and drop the downwind or downcurrent anchor.

To pick up the multi-decoy rig, simply reverse this process. Haul up the downwind anchor and work upwind, pulling the mother line in and detaching decoys as they come into the boat. Most veteran multi-rig users have some system for wrapping the mother line around pegs or a garden hose rack to keep it from tangling.

With this basic design, hunters can devise their own multiple-decoy rigs. One key is to make the anchor line (length of mother line from the anchor to the first decoy) approximately twice as long as expected water depth. If you intend to use your multi-decoy lines in varying depths, plan the anchor line length for the deepest depth.

There are many options in terms of different hardware—varying intervals between drop line attachments, varying length of drop lines, etc. By following the basic "blueprint" above, hunters can customize their multi-decoy rig to suit their specific hunting site.

Decoy Bags

Decoy bags have come a long way from the old days of toting decoys in burlap sacks. The best modern decoy bags are constructed from rip-stop polyester mesh, which is very durable and will drain easily. Modern decoy bags are also rot-proof. They are lightweight. They are available in different sizes, including extra-large bags that hold up to 48 standard decoys. They come in camouflage, drab, and white colors (the latter for snow geese). They open and close easily with grommeted draw cords or zippers. They have shoulder and waist straps for backpacking. Some decoy bags even float.

Hunters should be careful about backpacking too many decoys to a secluded hunting spot. Three dozen or more decoys toted over muddy terrain is a load. One-and-one-half or two dozen decoys is a more

reasonable burden, and this number is usually
sufficient to draw ducks to quiet backwaters. Choose a
bag designed to accommodate this smaller number of
decoys so that they will ride high on the back instead
of down low in a partially-filled bag, which makes
walking more difficult.

In recent years, manufacturers have begun selling specialty ponchos and slings for carrying silhouette, rag, and windsock decoys. These are worth the
money for hunters who hunt frequently in fields and
will hold dozens of these decoys at once, which saves
much time when setting decoys out or picking them up.

Chapter 7

Care and Repair

Before the start of each new waterfowl season, I have what I call my "bring 'em back to life" session. This is when I restore old decoys to good health. I drain water, seal leaks, touch up paint jobs, replace anchor lines and weights, and perform other chores to get last year's "wounded" decoys ready to return to work.

At the end of the season, my decoys are divided into two groups. The first group includes decoys that don't need any maintenance. My partners and I stack these in the blind and forget about them until it's time to put them back out the following fall. (We hunt on a private farm where access is controlled and the likelihood of theft is minimal.)

Next are the cripples. These are the ones we've taken out of the spread because they were sinking or had paint flaking off or other sundry damage. Throughout the season, we pile such decoys on the bank where we keep our boat tied. Then when the season is over, we carry these invalids home and store them in the barn until resurrection time, usually in late summer.

Actually, I look forward to this chore. It's a time of anticipation, sort of a kickoff for the new season. One of my hunting buddies helps me, and as we work we share memories of past hunts and hopes for future ones.

Store decoys by hanging them from lines on a garage wall or from rafters.

We work on a bench arranged from saw horses and sawmill boards. We retrieve the decoys from the barn, spread them in the grass, and inspect each one for damage. Some are beyond repair, and these wind up in the sinkhole. But most will have their mud cleaned away, their shot holes sealed, and their colors freshened up. Then after the sealer and paint dry, we tie on new strings and anchors and bag the decoys up, ready to be hauled back to the "front line" to rejoin the veterans in the spread. If decoys could talk to each other, I can imagine their conversation during this reunion.

"Hey, old buddy, I can't believe it's you. I'd given you up for a goner."

"I thought I was gone when that rookie in the blind opened up last year. Steel pellets were flying everywhere. Then that crippled greenhead swam behind me; I knew I was in trouble. Took four No. 2s in the side. Started taking water immediately. I was about to sink when they pulled me out of the spread and took me to the boat landing. But now I'm patched up and ready to go back in. How'd the season go after I left?"

"It was rough. Big Al and Mike popped main seams when the freeze hit, and they sank when the ice melted. Bitsy got her bill busted off when one of the hunters swung a push pole at a crippled gadwall. Strings broke on a couple of drakes I didn't know, and they drifted away on high water. Then several decoys got shot and taken out like you."

"Any news about reinforcements for this season?"

"Yeah, I heard we're getting a couple dozen new super mags with swivel heads. I hope they put 'em around the edges of the landing hole, where most of the cripple shooting occurs. As for me, I plan to just hunker down in the middle of the spread and keep my head low. I've been here for four seasons, and I've seen a lot of action. My paint's fading, and my sides are getting brittle."

"Well, luck to you, buddy. Keep her afloat."

"Yeah, luck to you too. Hope you don't get your tail caught in a quack."

Storing Decoys Between Seasons

Modern duck and goose decoys are very durable and resistant to extremes of temperature, light, etc. Still, decoys will last longer if cared for properly, especially during the warm months between hunting seasons. Following are storage tips to ensure long decoy life and service.

Before storing, clean decoys thoroughly to remove mud and grime. Fresh mud is easier to remove than mud that's baked onto decoys through the summer. This is why cleaning decoys at the end of one season saves time and elbow grease at the start of the next. Clean decoys by dry brushing with a stiff bristle brush or by pressure washing to remove caked-on mud. Then allow decoys to dry thoroughly before storing.

During the storage period, sunlight (ultraviolet rays) and heat are the two main enemies of molded-plastic (hollow-body) decoys. Prolonged exposure to sun and/or high temperatures will cause plastic decoys to become brittle, thus increasing the risk of breakage or seam failure. Also, exposure to ultraviolet rays will cause paint to fade and decoys to lose the sheen that live ducks have.

This is why plastic decoys should be stored in shady, relatively cool areas. One of the best ways to store them is to string them on clothesline wire (run the wire through the holes in the decoys' keels), then nail or tie these decoy-laden wires along an inside wall or in the rafters of a well-ventilated garage.

A good alternative to stringing decoys on wire is to pack them into mesh decoy bags, then hang the bags on nails along the garage wall. This allows for good ventilation for both the decoys and the bags.

The wrong way to store plastic decoys through summer is to pile them in a barn loft or attic where temperatures can become extreme, or to leave them exposed to the sun. Also, rats and mice are prone to chew on decoys that are stacked in an outbuilding inhabited by these rodents. Instead, decoys should be stored where these pests can't reach them.

Decoy Maintenance and Repair

"Modern duck and goose decoys are expensive to buy, and each old or damaged decoy you can repair and return to your spread saves several dollars," says Bob Holmes of Trenton, Tennessee. Holmes has been repairing and painting decoys for forty years. In the process, he has learned many tricks for restoring old or damaged decoys to usable condition. Now, each year he refurbishes dozens of decoys for his own spread and for those of friends.

Holmes says, "If location, concealment, and calling are equal, having a really good looking set of decoys will give a hunter an advantage over others whose decoys aren't as lifelike."

Following are Holmes's methods for restoring new life to plastic hollow-body decoys that are shot, busted, faded, or otherwise rendered unusable.

Repairing Shot Holes, Cracks, and Splits

Decoys leak through puncture holes (usually caused by misguided shot), from cracks in the body, or from splits along the seams where the molded decoy halves are joined.

The best time to find small leaks is while a decoy still has water in it. Squeeze the decoy and rotate it, watching for streams, drips, or bubbles of water forced out under pressure through the leak holes. Mark each hole for repair.

After making a thorough inspection, drill out each leak hole with a ⅛-inch drill bit. (A cordless electric drill is very handy for this purpose.) Drill the holes

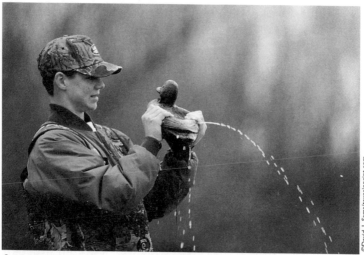

Squeeze the decoy to check it for leaks.

through the wall of the decoy precisely on the leaks. The purpose of drilling is to enlarge the leak holes so that silicone material can be squeezed inside the decoy to form stronger patches.

After all leaks have been found and drilled, drill a hole in the very tip of the decoy's tail. Then set the decoy in a rack with the tail pointed down to drain remaining water. Leave it in this position for a couple of days to allow the decoy to totally drain and dry out inside.

The next step is patching the drilled-out leak holes. The best patching material is a styrene-based silicone sealant named Lexel. This sealant accepts paint better than acetate-based silicone sealants.

Lexel should be applied to decoys with a standard caulking gun. The best caulking gun is an inexpensive model with a trigger latch that releases pressure immediately when the trigger is relaxed. This is much better than the more expensive model caulking gun that has a serrated, ratchet-type arm for holding pressure on the tube of sealant. The problem with such a gun is that it continues leaking sealant after the trigger is released.

Press the cartridge tip firmly against a drilled-out hole and apply Lexel, forcing some inside the decoy body to make an interior plug. Then use moistened fingertips to spread Lexel around the outside of the hole, smoothing it into a slight mound that completely covers the hole and tapers out onto the decoy's outer surface. All drilled-out holes should be repaired in this manner. Then the decoy should be set aside for three days before painting so that the Lexel can harden.

After this hardening period, patched decoys should be rechecked for leaks that may have been missed. Hold a patched decoy with the bottom toward your stomach, fingers on the back and thumbs on the decoy's bottom. Squeeze firmly. If resistance cannot be felt against the thumbs, a leak still exists. Such small leaks may be detected by squeezing and listening carefully or by feeling escaping air on your cheek. Sometimes it takes two or three such inspections to find and repair all leaks in a decoy.

Don't set freshly patched decoys in bright sunlight. If the decoys warm, air inside them will expand and blow the patches out. Instead, patch decoys in the afternoon, after the maximum daily temperature is reached, then set them in shade (carport, garage, barn, etc.) so that the Lexel can harden overnight.

Cracks and splits are repaired in a similar manner, except these require more drilling and filling because the leaks are larger. First drill holes at both ends of a crack or split. Then drill holes along both sides of the crack or split, approximately 1 inch apart and ¼ to ½ inch from the break. Next, after allowing the decoy to drain and dry, apply Lexel liberally into and over each hole. Then fill the crack or split with Lexel. Use moistened fingertips to connect and smooth all applications of Lexel into one broad patch, then set the decoy aside so that the Lexel can harden.

Major repairs, like replacing a broken bill or filling a large hole in the decoy, should be done with a two-part epoxy putty such as Sonic Weld. (Make sure to use epoxy putty, not liquid epoxy.) Epoxy putty can be mixed and mashed out like pie crust to cover holes or serve as a bonding agent for broken-off parts.

If a decoy is leaking but no holes can be found by squeezing and inspecting, take a close look at the plug in the injection-molding hole. This hole is usually beneath the decoy's tail. Sometimes slow leaks develop around this hole. Covering the molding hole with Lexel and working it in with your fingertips should repair these.

Also, subtle leaks may result from small cracks in the front or back of the keel. If cracks are found in the keel, drill and patch as described above.

Brightening and Painting

Decoys invariably lose their "new look" after a season or two of use. Exposure to sunlight will cause paint to fade. Banging and scraping against anchors, boat gunnels, ice, and other hard surfaces will chip paint off. Patches such as those described above require repainting. You should faithfully repaint decoys to keep them fresh and lifelike in appearance.

To do so, you will need color and feather pattern guides for accurate painting references. Taxidermy-mounted ducks are perfect for this purpose. Another good source is the book *Field Guide to Birds* by Roger

Tory Peterson. And a third excellent reference source is *Ducks Unlimited* magazine, which features close-up photographs of ducks and geese. Old issues may be scoured for high-quality photos of a broad range of species.

Decoys may be touched up quickly by highlighting prominent areas, or they may be totally repainted. This should be determined by how much time a hunter has and what shape his decoys are in. In either case, a fresh paint job should emphasize bright colors and high contrasts. Sharp distinctions between areas of dark and light will show up better to circling ducks and geese.

©Glenn D. Chambers, DU

Touching up decoys between seasons can be fun—and educational.

Before painting, however, decoys must be cleaned thoroughly. Dusty decoys should be brushed with a tampico fiber tire brush (wooden handle whitewall brush). Do not wet decoys; brush them while dry.

Decoys that are covered in mud, dried algae, pond scum, etc., must be washed with a pressure washer. One good way to do this is to take them to a car wash.

Spray several at a time in a mesh decoy bag. If you don't have such a bag, tie the decoys together with heavy cord or electrical wire through their anchor line holes. This will prevent the decoys from being pushed away by the high-pressure stream of water. After washing, decoys should be allowed to dry for twenty-four to forty-eight hours before painting.

Touch-ups for Mallard Decoys

Mallards are by far the most prevalent decoys in most hunters' spreads. Following is how to do a quick, simple touch-up on mallard decoys to restore their bright look.

Purchase one small- to medium-sized can of satin finish black latex paint and another can of satin-finish white latex paint. (Make sure to purchase satin finish, not gloss or semi-gloss. Satin finish has just the right luster for painting decoys.) Also, purchase a small assortment of brushes 1 inch wide and less. Brushes with exploded-tip nylon bristles are best. Artists' brushes are usually too soft to work with the rough finish on decoys.

Separate decoys according to sex, and work on the hens in one session and the drakes in another session.

To touch up a mallard hen, use a small brush to lengthen and widen the two white wing bars on each side of the body (bordering the speculum). Paint these wing bars so that they are approximately twice as wide as their original paint job (i.e., ¼ inch wide instead of ⅛ inch wide, etc.).

Next add white paint on the upper rear tail feathers. The best way to do this is by dry brushing. Load a small amount of paint on the brush, then make repeated light passes over the tailfeather area to impart streaks—not solid white. These two steps alone will add brightness and contrast to mallard hen decoys.

For mallard drake decoys, paint the top of the head and down the back of the neck with satin black. Dry brush the edges to feather the black into the green along the upper sides of the head. Paint the rump and tail feathers with satin black paint. Then set the decoys aside for the black paint to dry.

After the paint has dried, use white satin paint to enlarge and define the neckband (on live mallard drakes, this white ring is incomplete at the back of the neck),

©Bill Buckley

The touched-up decoy (left) looks bright and realistic, and will attract real ducks much more effectively than its faded cousin.

the wing bars bordering the speculum, the crescents behind the legs, and the upper rear tail feathers. Again, upper rear tail feathers should be dry brushed so that they are streaky rather than solid white.

Take a black permanent magic marker to highlight the nail (bump on the tip of the beak) and the nasal openings on the upper bill. Also, the black marker may be used to add thin black wing bars inside the white wing bars. Real mallards have two sets of color bars bordering the speculum—white on the outside and black on the inside.

Last, use model builder's black lacquer marker to add a gloss finish to the eyes.

Touching up decoys in this manner is a time-consuming, tedious process. Mallard drakes require approximately twice as much time as hens, since more detail is required.

Total Repainting

Sometimes rather than a touch-up, decoys may require total repainting. Their original paint might be flaked or faded, or a hunter might wish to repaint some decoys as other species to add variety and realism to his spread. (Standard-sized mallard hens can be repainted as gadwall or bluebills, pintail hens as wigeon, etc.)

The best way to totally repaint decoys is to purchase a Herter's decoy paint kit and follow the instructions that come with the kit. Decoys should be cleaned thoroughly before painting, and areas for different colors should be marked with a pencil.

There are three methods for getting paint to adhere better to hollow plastic decoys. The first and best method is to prime decoys with Kilz latex primer. Knock off as much old, scaly paint as possible by brushing with a tampico fiber brush. Then paint on a coating of Kilz primer and set the decoys aside to dry before repainting with natural colors.

Those who don't have the time or inclination to prime decoys can wash them in a fifty-fifty mixture of white distilled vinegar and water. This can be done with a paintbrush or by totally immersing decoys in this mixture. In either case, thoroughly wet the decoys and set them aside to dry.

The third method is to rub decoys vigorously with deglosser or liquid sandpaper (available at most home-supply stores). Latex deglosser or liquid sandpaper is better than oil-based deglosser, but the latter will work if the former isn't available.

Decoys prepared via any of these three methods and then totally painted shouldn't need repainting for two to three years, and then only touch-ups should be needed. Thus total repainting takes a lot of time and effort, but it pays long-term dividends.

Two Quick Tips for Decoy Color Renovation

Hunters might consider two other methods for returning natural sheen to weather-faded decoys.

The first is to dab petroleum jelly onto an old white sock and polish the heads of drake mallards, canvasbacks, redheads, and other species. Literally rub the jelly into the decoys' heads like polishing shoes. This will cause chalky, faded paint to come alive. The second method is to add a light coat of Armor-All to decoys before storing them for the summer. Clean the decoys thoroughly, washing them if necessary. Then after the decoys are dry, apply a light coating of Armor-All with a wet sock. This will lock the colors in and keep them from bleaching out.

Chapter 8

Decoy Tips

A waterfowl decoy encyclopedia still couldn't include all the gimmicks, tips, and tricks used by North America's duck and goose hunters. Innovation is one of the great companions in this sport. Members of each hunting partnership usually do something different from everybody else, something they have devised to solve a problem or make a decoy spread look better. Discovering and comparing these personal touches is one of the enjoyable aspects of getting to accompany many different hunters around the country, which I do.

Following is a miscellaneous collection of decoy tips for you to assess and possibly add to your own hunting situations.

Ducks on a log

In a swamp or marsh setting, if a log is present, some ducks will invariably climb up on it for resting and preening. This is why hunters should pull a log to the edge of their decoy spread and line up several full-body standup decoys (like Flambeau Enticers) on it. If the wind is blowing, use a hammer and small nails to secure the decoys' bases to the log. These decoys, on the log and out of the water, will be visible, realistic, and serene-looking to circling ducks. This is an especially good idea for permanent spreads, where decoys are left out through the season.

Dipping jugs to make black decoys

Black plastic jugs may not have much aesthetic appeal in a decoy spread, but they certainly fool the ducks. Solid black jugs (two- or three-liter soft drink containers, gallon milk jugs, etc.) are great for catching ducks' attention at long distances. These are most frequently used in large open-water spreads, mixed in with standard decoys, and are an inexpensive means of adding numbers and visibility to a spread. (In some areas, using jugs as decoys is prohibited. Check local regulations before adding jugs to your spread.)

The best way to cover jugs is to dip them in a mixture of cold roofing pitch (available at any building center), gasoline, and acetone. This is a simple but messy procedure. Wear old clothes and rubber gloves that can be discarded after the jugs are dipped.

For several seasons' use, plastic jugs' sides should be roughed up with coarse sandpaper so that the black pitch will adhere better. However, most hunters who use jugs will dip slick-sided jugs, then redip them between seasons to cover areas where the black pitch has worn off.

The best place to dip jugs is in the yard or in a field where no damage will be incurred by dripping pitch. (Do not dip jugs in a garage or on a concrete surface.)

In a five-gallon plastic bucket, pour approximately two gallons of black pitch, then add enough gasoline (stirred in with a paint mixing paddle) to make a mixture the consistency of thick latex paint. Next stir in a few ounces of acetone, which will etch the plastic and help the pitch adhere to it.

After the pitch mixture is ready, dip the jugs by hand one at a time, completely covering each jug. Add more pitch, gasoline, and acetone as necessary to keep enough mixture in the bucket to submerge the jugs. As the jugs are dipped, line them up in the grass or string them on a clothesline and leave them a couple of days for drying.

More black duck decoys

If you hunt where black ducks are common, consider repainting half of your mallard hen decoys as black ducks. These will show up better at long distances, plus they are good as confidence decoys for wary black ducks and mallards. Experience has shown that a spread with numerous black duck decoys will be more effective at attracting ducks than a same-size spread with few or no black duck decoys.

Using silhouette decoys in shallow water

Silhouette duck or goose decoys may be used in shallow-water spreads. Cut PVC pipe sections and job them into the mud. (Cut one end diagonally to form a point for pushing into the mud.) Then push the pipe sections down so that the top edge is close to the water's surface. Insert decoy stakes into pipe sections to hold the silhouettes upright.

Getting the range

Use a laser rangefinder for learning precise distances when setting decoys around a blind. Set decoys or drive poles at 35 yards, then shooters will have an accurate reference for when waterfowl are in lethal range.

Weighted keels from unweighted

Weighted-keel decoys offer one main advantage over water-keel models: When tossed on the water, they will right themselves. However, weighted-keel decoys are significantly more expensive than water-keel decoys.

Hunters can have the convenience of weighted-keel decoys for the price of water keels by converting the latter to the former. Simply fill the keels with sand, then plug the end of the keels with silicone sealant and wait a few hours for the sealant to harden. These altered decoys will function as well as factory-made weighted-keel decoys.

Divers add to spread's visibility

When hunting open marshes, rivers, or lakes, consider adding a few bluebill or canvasback decoys on the outside edge of your spread. Even if you aren't hunting divers, these brightly colored decoys will draw more attention to your spread from passing mallards, pintails, etc.

Retrieving decoys from the bank

Hunters who don't have a boat can still toss out decoys and hunt over a pond that's too deep to wade to retrieve the decoys. This task can be accomplished by screwing several long screws at different angles into a 6-ounce lead sinker. Leave ¾ inch of each screw protruding from the weight. Then attach 50 feet of stout nylon line to the weight and wrap the line around a stick to keep it from tangling when not in use.

When it's time to retrieve the decoys, unwind the line, then toss the weight just in front of each decoy's head. As the weight sinks, it will fall across the decoy's anchor line. As the weight is pulled back to the bank, the screws will snag the line and pull the decoy in with the weight.

Use float board to deflect current

When multi-rigging (trotlining) decoys in a river or tidal marsh with strong current, attach a "float board" to the decoy line ahead of the first upcurrent decoy. This board, a 3-foot square of flat-black plywood, will break the current so that the decoys can float naturally behind it. Up to a dozen decoys can be strung out behind the board.

Do away with the orange

Some mallard decoys have bright orange legs, and for reasons known only to muskrats, these rodents like to chew on these orange legs, which causes leaks. Thus hunters who include such decoys in a permanent spread (left out through the season) in a marsh or slough where muskrats live should paint the legs a dark color, such as gray or brown. When the orange color is covered, the muskrats ignore the decoys.

Pack frame makes packing decoys easier

For backpacking duck decoys, purchase an aluminum backpack frame (try local yard sales) and attach your decoy bag to it with plastic cable ties. Then fill the bag with decoys, adjust the frame straps, and take off. A frame makes carrying a full bag of decoys much easier than backpacking solely with the straps on the bag.

Oversight, overflight

When field-hunting geese, the caller(s) should call from the upwind edge of the spread. Also, kites and

Motion decoys like these windsocks should be positioned close to the caller.

other motion decoys should be positioned close to the callers. This causes incoming geese to focus their attention in this area and hopefully overlook the downwind or middle portion of the spread where the shooters are lying.

Yellow is the color...

When hunting in a shallow flooded cornfield, paint decoy anchors yellow. It looks like corn to waterfowl flying over the field, but it is fully legal, the same as using plastic corn.

Notch boat paddle to pick up decoys

Instead of leaning over in a boat to retrieve decoys, cut a notch in the edge of a boat paddle, and use the paddle as a hook to pick up decoys by their anchor strings.

Give 'em the hook

Another good way to retrieve decoys from a boat is with a homemade hook. Go to a building supply center and purchase a 6-foot dowel rod (1 or 1½ inches thick). Screw a screw-in hook into the end of the rod. This device will greatly speed picking up decoys on a river or open lake.

Do the wave for snow geese

Success: This hunter carries out more than the decoys she came in with.

To create movement in a field spread for snow geese, erect a tall pole (10 feet or higher) with a 150-foot-long string attached to its top in the center of the spread. Every 5 feet along the string tie a white rag. When geese are approaching, stretch the line out crosswind and pull the line up and down in an undulating motion. The rags on the line will rise and fall like geese looking for a landing spot. Keep doing this until the geese are close enough to shoot.

Do the wave—part II

Another way to impart movement to a goose spread—snows or Canadas—is to place several "flags" throughout the spread. Cut out and paint several head-shaped stakes and staple lightweight cloth or Tyvek squares to them (white for snow geese, black for

211

Canadas). When the wind blows these flags will flutter much like the movement of feeding geese.

Slide decoys instead of packing them

Sliding decoys behind you may be easier than backpacking them in muddy terrain, shallow water, snow, etc. In gooey mud or shallow water (ricefields, etc.), skid decoys behind you in a kayak or small layout boat. These boats will slide easily on wet ground, even with a heavy load, whereas backpacking such a load would push the packer into the mire with each step.

Reeling and rocking

When ducks are circling a spread suspiciously, use a short fishing rod and reel rigged with heavy monofilament to reel a decoy through the open landing hole. When the decoy is halfway through the hole, stop reeling and twitch it like working a big topwater bait. This will cause the decoy to rock and bob, adding life-like motion to the spread. Then resume reeling to swim the decoy in front of the blind.

Keep 'er afloat

To keep a mesh decoy bag from sinking, put some foam object inside it: a retriever dummy, cooler top, flotation cushion, etc. Such an object will keep the bag on the surface after the last decoy is retrieved from it and is being set out by the hunter.

Bleach bottle goose decoys

Cost-conscious hunters can convert one-gallon bleach bottles into goose decoys with minimal time, effort, and expense. Use a power saw to cut angled blocks off a two-by-four for heads. Drill a hole in the bottom of the head and use wood glue to secure a 15-

inch length of 7/16 inch dowel rod in the hole. Then cut holes near the base of the jug, and push the dowel rod through to position the head. Paint the decoy according to the species being hunted.

Felt like geese

To add realism to goose decoys, cover the heads and necks with black felt. The felt reflects sunlight just like the feathers of real geese.

Sign on the dotted line

To affix your name to plastic decoys, use a liquid-paper correct-type pen. The white shows up well, dries quickly, and is more durable than felt-tip markers.

Appendix

The following is a list of the waterfowling guides and decoy manufacturers referenced in the book.

Waterfowling Guides

Billy Adams
21221 Winfree Avenue
Petersburg, VA 23803
Phone: 804-526-8464

Harry Boyle
460 Pallisades Drive
Chico, CA 95928
Phone: 530-342-0617

Mark Burch
407 East Main Street
Humansville, MO 65674
Phone: 417-754-8379

Bruce "Whicker Bill" Crist
P.O. Box 873
Ft. Pierre, SD 57532
Phone: 605-224-0681

Larry Davis
6860 Bayshore Road
Marblehead, OH 43440
Phone: 419-732-3930

Don Jensen
Box 1373 Cardston,
AL POK OKO
Phone: 403-653-1737
403-653-1893

Greg Karnes Sportman's Lodge
Sifton, Manitoba
(U.S. sddress: 4926 Harvest Lane
Bloomington, IN 47404)
Phone: 800-304-5800

Don Stavinoha
15 Garden Oak
Columbus, TX 78934
Phone: 979-732-6996

Tony Toye
Big River Guide Service
43605 County Hwy. E.
Boscobel, WI 53805
Phone: 605-375-7447
E-mail: toyedecoys@tds.net

Decoy Manufacturers

Avery Outdoors, Inc.
335 Cumberland Street
Memphis, TN 38112
Phone: 901-324-1500
www.averyoutdoors.com

Blackwater Decoy Company
913 East Main Street
Newark, OH 43056
Phone: 888-BWDECOY
(888-293-3269)
www.duckdecoys.com

Decoys

Big Foot Decoys
Clinton Decoy Company
P.O. Box 3093
Clinton, IA 52732
Phone: 319-242-8801
www.jdv.net/bigfoot

Cabela's
400 East Avenue A
Oshkosh, NE 69190
Phone: 800-237-4444
www.cabelas.com

Carry-Lite Decoys
Carry-Lite, Inc.
5203 W. Clinton Avenue
Milwaukee, WI 53223
Phone: 414-355-3520
www.carrylite-decoy.com

Expedite International
1632 Livingstone Road
Hudson, WI 54016
Phone: 715-381-2935
www.trumotion.com

Fatal de DUCKtion
Mathews Motorized Decoys
8800 Mathews Lane
Marysville, CA 95901
Phone: 530-742-0743
www.motormallard.com

Feather Flex Decoys
c/o Outland Sports
P.O. Box 220
Neosho, Mo 64850
Phone: 417-451-4438
www.outland-sports.com

Final Approach Blinds
Ron Latschaw
1877 Hubbard Lane
Grants Pass, OR 97527
Phone: 541-476-7562
www.finalapproachblinds.com

Flagman Products
c/o Randy Bartz
1215 West Center St.
Oronoco, MN 55960
Phone: 507-367-4782
www.flagmanproducts.com

Flambeau Products
Corporation
P.O. Box 97
15981 Valplast Road
Middlefield, OH 44062
Phone: 800-457-5252
www.flambeau.com

Flapperz
Division of Wingman, Inc.
P.O. Box 271
Douglas, MI 49406
Phone: 888-33WINGS
(888-339-4647)

Fowl Foolers Decoys
Bay Area Products, Inc.
4942 Fremont Road (Rt. 53)
Port Clinton, OH 43452
Phone: 419-732-2147

G&H Decoy, Inc.
P.O. Box 1208
Henryetta, OK 74437
Phone: 800-GHDECOY
(800-443-3269)
www.ghdecoys.com

Appendix

Hunter's Specialties
6000 Huntington Court, NE
Cedar Rapids, IA 52402
Phone: 800-728-0321
www.hunterspec.com

Herter's
P.O. Box 426
Greenville, NC 27835-0426
Phone: 800-654-3825
www.herters.com

Higdon Motion Decoys, Inc.
7 Universal Way
Metropolis, IL 62960
Phone: 618-524-3385
www.higdondecoys.com

Mallard Machine
C/O Rob Brock
700 Drake Street
Bentonville, AR 72712
Phone: 502-770-3825
www.themallardmachine.com

Outlaw Decoys
624 N. Fancher Road
Spokane, WA 99219
Phone: 800-653-3269
www.outlaw.com

Pulsator Decoy
Paducah Shooters Supply
3919 Cairo Road
Paducah, KY 42001
Phone: 270-442-3242
www.pssguns.com

Real Decoy
A&M Waterfowl, Inc.
P.O. Box 102
Ripley, TN 38063
Phone: 901-635-4003
www.realdecoy.com

Real Geese
**Webfoot-Licensed Specialty
Products, Inc.**
3177 E. U.S. Route 20
Fremont, OH 43420
Phone: 419-334-4260
www.webfootdecoys.com

RoboDuk
10198 Hwy. 70
Marysville, CA 95901
Phone: 530-743-8322
www.Roboduk.com

Tanglefree Industries
1261 Heavenly Drive
Martinez, CA 94553
Phone: 800-982-4868
www.tanglefree.com

Texas Hunting Products, Inc.
P.O. Box 440296
Houston, TX 77244
Phone: 800-346-1005
www.texashunting.com

Wonderduck Decoys
505 North Price
Marshall, TX 75670
Phone: 800-876-1697
www.wonderduck.com